SOUTHE[I]

TO THE COAS[T]

Images from the Transport Treasury Collection

Compiled by Jeffery Grayer

The
· Transport ·
Treasury

© Images and design: The Transport Treasury 2021. Text Jeffery Grayer

ISBN 978-1-913251-18-5

First published in 2021 by Transport Treasury Publishing Ltd., 16 Highworth Close, High Wycombe, HP13 7PJ

www.ttpublishing.co.uk

Printed in the UK by Henry Ling Limited at the Dorset Press, Dorchester. DT1 1HD

Front Cover: Steam to the Kent coast personified in this view of Battle of Britain pacific No. 34089 *602 Squadron* seen at the platform end at Ramsgate having arrived with a service from London. When new, just 3 years and 2 months before the date of this image, which was taken on 2 February 1952, the pacific was allocated to Ramsgate shed. It was to be reallocated to Stewarts Lane in May 1951 and after rebuilding at the end of 1960 was to last in service until the very end of Southern steam in July 1967 with its final allocation being Salisbury. When it became apparent that work for these new 4-6-2s could readily be found on the south eastern section of the SR it was felt appropriate to name them after airfields, personalities and squadrons associated with the Battle of Britain which had been fought largely over the skies of this area. Although 602 Squadron had their home in Scotland they moved south in 1940 and were based at a number of airfields in Sussex and Kent including Kenley and Biggin Hill, both of which, of course, were to be commemorated in the names of other members of the Battle of Britain class. *RCR4348*

Frontispiece: The delightful signal box at Sidmouth, seen here on 13 July 1960, continued in use until the closure of the line to passengers in March 1967. It dated from the opening of the branch by the Sidmouth Railway in 1874, although the line was worked by the LSWR from the outset, and contained a frame of 23 levers. It can be seen that the original timber superstructure on a brick base has been extended on the left of this view. The box remained relatively busy into the late 1950s and early 1960s handling 31 passenger departures and arrivals on weekdays in the winter of 1958/59 for example which included one through service to/from Waterloo. Not all of the local services went through to Sidmouth Junction as there were a couple of short workings to/from Tipton St. Johns where connections were made with services to/from Exmouth. In the years following the introduction of DMUs in November 1963 the daily service was subsequently reduced and by the time of the final summer timetable in 1966 there were just 7 departures from Sidmouth Junction increasing to 11 departures on Saturdays. Coal traffic continued for a few weeks after passenger closure until 8 May 1967 after which the line was completely closed. Although much of the infrastructure of the terminus survives into the present day, sadly the signal box was subsequently demolished as no alternative use could be found. *RCR14991*

Opposite: The summer crowds have not yet arrived at Hayling Island terminus and judging by the fact that home going commuters and shoppers making their way down the station approach road are wrapped up with duffle coats and raincoats, and that hats and scarves are well in evidence, the weather on 14 April 1960, the date of this view, was none too warm. A1X No. 32678 is in the process of running round its train following its short 13 minute run from the main line junction at Havant. Turnround times at the terminus were generally tight on this intensively worked service with only seven minutes often being allowed. Two taxicabs wait apparently in vain for custom alongside a Triumph Herald and a bicycle but it would appear that the majority of the passengers will be using shanks's pony for their onward journey although there was a convenient bus stop located at the end of the station approach road. *AEB5255*

Rear Cover: The passage of a pair of R1 tank locomotives is reflected in the calm waters of Folkestone Harbour whilst several small craft lie at anchor. The two 0-6-0Ts, Nos. 31128 and 31337, make their way steadily up the incline to the main line at Folkestone Junction ready for their next banking turn. The R Class veteran 0-6-0Ts were to a Stirling design dating from 1887, thirteen of which were subsequently modified by Wainwright between 1910 and 1922 to become Class R1. By the date of this image, 19 October 1954, only one had been withdrawn with No. 31128 lasting in service until 1959 and No. 31337 until 1960, one of the primary reasons for their retention being their suitability for banking duties at Folkestone. Whilst many tourists used Folkestone Harbour, which was the departure point for cross Channel services to Boulogne, Calais and Ostend, many holidaymakers stayed in the town itself with the surrounding area catering for numerous visitors well into the 1950s and early 1960s. Following cessation of ferry services in 2001 and after years of decline for traditional Victorian seaside resorts generally, Folkestone has experienced something of a renaissance of late, particularly in the arts, with considerable redevelopment taking place around the harbour area. *RCR5588*

Contents

Introduction

Every January, for a number of years, British Railways (BR) published weighty annual travel guides, in excess of 500 pages and keenly priced at 1/6d (7½p) in 1958 for example, entitled "Holiday Haunts" which in five volumes covered different geographical areas of the country. This title had originally been used by the Great Western Railway (GWR) from 1923-29 in the annual publication of their own guidebooks. Volume No. 5 in the BR series featured Southern England from Kent to Cornwall together with the Channel Islands. Leafing through the guide one could see sepia illustrations of resorts, descriptions of local attractions and advertisements giving details of accommodation. These ranged from grand establishments such as the Fircroft Hotel in Boscombe with a range of features including a hard tennis court, putting green, ballroom, hotel cinema, dancing and orchestra ranging in price from 10 - 13½ guineas weekly in the summer season, sadly demolished in 2010 and replaced with a block of flats, to the more modest guest houses such as the "Lyncliffe" in Lynton featuring "plenty of good food" and "H&C in all rooms" with terms from 5 guineas per week. There were also maps of railway routes and details of services to enable the holidaymaker to travel easily to the various resorts and to get around once there using the ever popular Holiday Runabout tickets giving unlimited travel within specified areas for a week for bargain fares starting from 18/6d (92½p).

Using this guide as a basis, some 80 resorts which were served by the Southern Region (SR) of BR have been identified and a selection of 50 of these is illustrated here with photographs from the vast Transport Treasury archive which currently numbers in excess of half a million images from the collections of a number of eminent contributing photographers including Leslie Freeman, Dick Riley, Anthony Bennett, and Alec Swain. A variety of motive power from many different classes is featured in the scenes shown here from main line express locomotives to humble tank engines. Many resorts such as St. Leonards, Ramsgate and Bournemouth played host to their own motive power depots and these ranged in size from those at the major sheds at places such as Brighton to the humbler single locomotive accommodation at several branch line termini and these are included here along with images of the ever popular holiday camping coach.

Whilst the SR of BR and its predecessor, the Southern Railway, were primarily known for their frequent electrified services which took commuters and visitors to the capital, they were equally noted for the many routes that took the holidaying public, and Londoners in particular, to the south, south east and south west coasts of the UK and for the named expresses that plied these routes. The "Atlantic Coast Express (ACE)", "Bournemouth Belle", "The Man of Kent" and "Royal Wessex" were just some of the famous trains which delivered the traveller to their destination in some style. From the east of Kent, epitomized in such resorts as Margate and Ramsgate, to the south coast hotspots of Brighton and Bournemouth, the east Devon resorts of Sidmouth and Exmouth and stretching to the far west at Bude and Padstow, the SR enabled the holidaymaker to reach his destination with often frequent and comfortable through services hauled over the years by steam, diesel and electric traction. In this book we take a look at the numerous resorts served by the SR from the large multi-platformed stations provided at places such as Brighton to the humbler termini to be seen at Allhallows-on-Sea, Seaton and Lyme Regis. In the south west the SR had to share the tourist trade spoils with the Western Region and drew the short straw serving as it did the less popular north Devon and Cornish coasts with their shorter holiday season rather than south Devon and Cornwall which enjoyed a lengthy tourist season with the balmier climate of the English Riviera.

The SR specialised in providing through coaches to many of the smaller destinations and this was epitomized in the multi-portioned "ACE" which at various times conveyed through coaches for Ilfracombe, Torrington, Bude, Padstow, Plymouth, Exmouth, Sidmouth, Seaton and Lyme Regis. Although this train would leave the capital with perhaps 12 or 13 coaches in tow behind a gleaming pacific locomotive the travellers for a particular destination often found themselves accommodated in just a one or two coach train by the time they had reached journey's end at some bucolic branch line terminus, often powered on the final few miles by a lowly vintage tank locomotive. The Southern Railway and its successor BR region did not waste the marketing opportunity afforded by the naming of several of the West Country Class locomotives. There were many examples named after seaside resorts served directly by rail such as 34008 "Padstow" and 34044 "Woolacombe", and several locations which did not boast a station such as 34039 "Boscastle" and 34093 "Saunton" but which could be reached easily by road from nearby stations. There were even resorts which formerly had enjoyed the benefit of rail connection such as 34038 "Lynton" and but which no longer saw any trains.

Following boundary changes in 1963 the SR west of Wilton was transferred to the Western Region and against the background of the swingeing cuts of the 1960s the SR's tourist lines in both the far south west and in east Devon were decimated and today former SR rails serve only Barnstaple and Exmouth. However, the majority of the major resorts of the south coast today continue to enjoy frequent train services although of course the variety of 60 years ago is no longer apparent in the uniform, rather dull trains of today. There have been some casualties even here with the closure of the Swanage branch, although

subsequently re-opened by a preservation society, and of lines to Ventnor, Cowes, Hayling Island, Hythe and Allhallows-on-Sea. I have taken a somewhat liberal interpretation of the word "Coast" in that a few estuarine resorts such as Topsham on the River Exe, Barnstaple on the River Taw, Instow on the River Torridge and Wadebridge on the River Camel have been included in this selection. The Isle of Wight resorts have been deliberately omitted as they are featured in the companion volume "Isle of Wight Railway Art".

This unashamedly nostalgic collection looks back at the stations, locomotives and stock that could be seen in the 1950s and early 1960s at a variety of resorts served by the SR. These destinations appealed both to day trippers and longer term holidaymakers delighting in what might be called the mass tourism of the "kiss me quick" and "bucket and spade" brigades and to the discerning tourist wishing to sample perhaps the more select destinations on offer. To enhance this sense of nostalgia, introductory quotations from the 1958 edition of "Holiday Haunts" are provided for each of the resorts covered revealing, in an age of greater innocence and simpler pleasures, just what has been lost in the intervening 60 years and how true those famous opening lines of "The Go-Between" by L.P. Hartley are - *"The past is a foreign country : they do things differently there".*

Jeffery Grayer.   Devon 2021

Typifying the Southern express to the coast is Battle of Britain pacific No. 34072 *257 Squadron* captured near Chislehurst on 6 April 1955 storming along in fine style at the head of "The Man of Kent". This named train, one of the principal services from London serving the Kent coast resorts and the last regular SR steam express to be named, began life in 1953 and lasted until June 1961. In the winter of 1958/59, for example, this train left London's Charing Cross station twice daily except Sundays and served the coastal resorts of Folkestone, Dover, Walmer, Deal, Sandwich, Ramsgate, Broadstairs and Margate. By the end of the 1950s the minimum loading was ten coaches with eleven or even twelve being necessary on occasions. The tight 80 minute schedule was taxing for the locomotive but as the trains were mainly worked by Bulleid light pacifics from Ramsgate shed by this time this proved to be well within their capabilities although the less powerful Schools class occasionally deputised. With the rundown of the steam fleet in the early 1960s this named train finished its life with diesel haulage in the shape of either single or paired D5000 or D6500 types. No. 34072 is fortunately still with us being currently located on the Swanage Railway. *RCR6011*

Kent

ALLHALLOWS-ON-SEA

38¾ miles from London served by frequent Southern Electric trains from Charing Cross with change of train at Gravesend Central. Journey time approx. 1½ hours.

Allhallows, although having its roots in antiquity, is in some respects one of our newer resorts. Situated on Kent's northern shore, where sea and countryside meet, the open fields, the views over the Isle of Grain, the sands and the safe bathing bring many visitors to its shore. From the plateau reached by the road from the station, both the Thames and the Medway rivers can be seen at the same time, as well as all kinds of shipping en route for London, the Medway ports, or the open sea. Allhallows has a bright future. Roads have been built and development into a pleasant rural resort is well on the way.

Above: Typical motive power in the shape of a Wainwright H Class 0-4-4T No. 31324 is seen at the platform end replenishing its tanks from the balloon water crane on the penultimate day of operation, 2 December 1961. This water crane remains the only railway artifact on the site, being currently surrounded by a caravan site. Judging by the unusual congregation at the platform end several people were taking their final trip on the branch. One of the few signs of the anticipated development of the resort is "The Pilot" hotel and public house seen in the left background. Unfortunately the public were not attracted to the resort, situated as it was on the muddy banks of the Thames estuary. The station was 400 yards from the "beach", more accurately designated "mud" on the OS map, and downstream from a sewer outfall. With the general decline of the British seaside resort the 1¾ mile branch, previously doubled from Stoke Junction, was singled and eked out an uneventful existence until closure in December 1961.
AEB5886

Opposite top: An interesting experiment is captured in this view of the terminus taken on 24 October 1953. A company called Associated Commercial Vehicles (ACV) built a rudimentary three car diesel unit in 1952 as a test project. ACV was a holding company formed in 1948 when AEC purchased Crossley Motors and the Maudsley Motor Company. They subsequently took control of the coachbuilding firm Park Royal Vehicles along with its subsidiary Charles H Roe. In 1962 ACV was bought by Leyland Motors. The railcars normally ran in a three car formation although they could operate as a single or two car unit. Trials were undertaken nationwide on various out of the way parts of the BR system including the Didcot to Newbury branch, the Amlwch branch in Anglesey and Dalmellington to Ayr in Scotland. The SR was given the opportunity to try the new unit and chose the Allhallows branch. A further image of this unit can be seen on page 95 of the companion volume in this series "Southern Medley". *RCR4851*

Above: The former single sided platform was converted to the island platform seen here in 1933 to cater for the expected crowds and a longer full width steel canopy provided. A small signal box was located on the platform. Some lengthy trains did operate in the 1930s and 1940s bringing in holidaymakers and day trippers and August Bank Holiday 1934 saw some 9,500 passengers arrive at this rather bleak destination. An estate company was established to develop the resort but the hopes of a new Southend-on-Sea arising were ultimately to be left unrealised and latterly two or three coach trains more than sufficed for the limited traffic, the population of Allhallows rising from 350 in 1930 to just 600 by 1960. Ironically today there is a sizeable population on the caravan site built on the site of the former station. H Class No. 31517, with a typical two coach set, is seen waiting to leave the terminus on 13th. August 1959 in which year there were still a generous eleven departures for the main line at Gravesend on weekdays, twelve on Saturdays and no less than fourteen on Sundays. *AEB5121*

SHEERNESS-ON-SEA

52¾ miles from London. Served by frequent express trains from London Victoria with change of train at Sittingbourne. Journey time approx.two hours.

Sheerness, in addition to its well known dockyard, has lovely pleasure gardens, an amusement park, open air swimming pool, a children's boating pool, a theatre and three cinemas. There are steamer cruises from the pier and the never-failing fascination of watching the stream of shipping, naval and mercantile, yachts and small craft, coming and going or passing by.

Above: Class H 0-4-4T No. 31158 has charge of the 11am Sittingbourne to Sheerness shuttle service and is seen here crossing the Kingsferry bridge on 16 August 1954. This Wainwright tank locomotive only had another six months to run before withdrawal from Gillingham shed in April the following year. The first railway bridge to cross the River Swale was constructed for the London, Chatham & Dover Railway (LC&DR) in 1860 being of the bascule type, a design which allowed it to open to permit large vessels to pass. It was replaced in 1960 by a combined seven span road and railway vertical lift bridge carrying a single track railway line, a two lane road and a footpath. It has a central lifting span permitting the passage of tall vessels and currently is raised a score of times daily. A new high level road bridge, Sheppey Crossing, opened nearby in 2006 which did away with the inconvenience to motorists caused by closure of the road when shipping passed underneath. *RCR5225*

Opposite top: The end of an era at Sheerness is portrayed in this 13 June 1959 view featuring Ivatt tank No. 41309 which had been allocated from new in 1952 to Faversham shed (73E). Phase 1 of the Kent Coast electrification would see the branch to Sheerness electrified from Monday 15th. June, spelling the end for steam powered services. As a consequence Faversham shed closed in June and the half dozen of these Midland Region 2-6-2Ts on their books would be transferred away to Ashford shed. The third rail and colour light signalling is in place ready for electric services and the signal box seen here had already been abolished from 24th. May when Sittingbourne power box took over control of the branch. Coach set 551 seen on the left is part of a Southern Region Mk1. Set. *RCR13643*

Opposite bottom: The new order is represented by 2 HAP, latterly Class 414, EMU No. 5621 seen at the terminus on 31 March 1965 having recently arrived and discharged its passengers. Electrification initially gave the town an hourly through service to London Victoria although after May 1973 the only through services were in the morning and evening peak hours for a number of years. The middle road seen above was removed in August 2004 during track relaying. No. 5621 was one of the first batch of thirty-six units which were built to the SR style Bulleid design using the reclaimed underframes of older 2NOL units. The 2 HAPs comprised a Driving Motor Brake Open Second (DMBSO) plus a Driving Trailer Composite with lavatory (DTCK). All were withdrawn by 1982 with the DMBSO being "refreshed" for integration into the class 415 refurbishment programme. *AS R68-2*

WHITSTABLE

59 miles from London. Served by frequent express trains from London Victoria with refreshment car on certain trains. Also served by the all Pullman "Kentish Belle".

Whitstable is a mixture of old and new. Its name of course indicates its ancient claim to fame, the oyster industry. During the oyster season it is fascinating to watch the picturesquely dressed dredgermen on the yawls or around the town. Whitstable has a long holiday season and those obliged to stagger their holidays will be well rewarded by longer days by the sea.

Opposite top: Opened in 1860 this was the original terminus station at Sheerness located half a mile from the town and serving the dockyard. In 1883 a new station opened, via a 0.6 mile long spur line from the throat of the terminus, with the suffix "On-Sea" to promote the location as a holiday resort. Trains were required to reverse from the dockyard station to the new station and vice versa upon return. During WW1 the new station was closed and all services called at the dockyard station until 1921 when a further spur was built thus creating a triangular junction to allow trains to run directly into the new station, the dockyard station then being converted into a goods depot following re-opening of the new station in January 1922. The dockyard station remained in use for goods traffic until May 1963. The Royal Navy departed Sheerness in 1960 and the dockyard subsequently closed although one line remained in use as a private siding until 1968. The dockyard station comprised two platforms at right angles to the single-storey brick main building with a slated pitched roof that contained the booking office and waiting room. The tracks were covered by a pitched overall roof. The above view of the boarded up station frontage was taken on 31 March 1965, the building being demolished in 1971. *AS R68-1*

Opposite bottom: A panoramic view of the grass grown layout at Sheerness Dockyard station seen in March 1965. Following demolition in 1971 the site was swallowed up by the construction of Sheerness Steel Works which also occupied the northern side of the triangular junction with the current terminus. The steel works was commissioned in 1972 and produced steel with the electric arc furnace method using scrap metal rather than by smelting iron ore. The Works closed in 2002, then re-opened and closed again in 2012. Demolition of the site has been undertaken in recent years to provide car parking for imported cars. *AS R67-5*

Above: Entering the curving platforms of Whitstable & Tankerton, the addition of this second location to the station name was in response to requests from property developers from the Tankerton area to the east of the town when the new station was opened in 1915. N Class mogul No. 31868 arrives with a service for London on Saturday 7 September 1958. The coach set carries roof boards and consists of Pullman stock so this is probably the 5 pm departure from Ramsgate which saw the return working of 1st and 2nd class Pullmans which had earlier formed the 11.35 am service from Victoria to Ramsgate. If this is so it is running very late as it was due at Whitstable at 5.42pm and, if the station clock is to be believed, it is now 7.05pm. Being charitable perhaps the clock was not working! This service was advertised in the timetable as "Including limited Pullman car facilities" so for payment of a supplement of 3/6 (17.5p) 1st. or 2/- (10p) 2nd. from both Herne Bay and Whitstable, returning holidaymakers and other travellers could journey up to London in style enjoying the luxury of "Refreshments served at every seat". *PH659*

Above: This view looking towards London shows the platform extensions fabricated from pre-cast concrete components which were installed to accommodate twelve car EMU stock introduced as part of the Kent Coast Electrification scheme. One of the twenty-four E5XXX locomotives, later designated Class 71, built in 1958 and designed to operate over the third rail and, with the aid of their pantographs, over sidings and non-electrified track where overhead wires were provided, is seen passing through with a short freight service. Although as mixed traffic locomotives they hauled prestige passenger trains such as the "Golden Arrow" and "Night Ferry", they found themselves allocated more and more to freight turns. Ten were converted in 1967/8 to Class 74 electro-diesels giving them more route flexibility but the original locomotives remained under utilised and withdrawal came in 1976/77. This view was taken from the overbridge carrying the former historic Canterbury & Whitstable (C&W) line on which passenger services had ceased in 1931. The final scheduled freight ran in 1952 although the line was briefly re-opened during the severe flooding of 1953 to enable traffic to bypass the breach in the main line between Whitstable and Faversham. *HW358*

The main object of interest to the visiting enthusiasts appears to be the steam roller parked on the former trackbed of the Canterbury & Whitstable (C&W) line seen here on the 18 March 1961. The C&W was the first railway to serve Whitstable opening in 1830 and some claim it to be the "first railway in Britain" although there are other contenders for this title. Taken over by the South Eastern Railway (SER) the line was never a money spinner and suffered competition when the LC&DR opened their line through the town from Faversham to Margate which afforded a much better service to London. The original Whitstable Harbour station was opened in 1830 located north of Harbour Street and was extended in length to take three carriages in 1870. However the shunting of wagons in the harbour area was impeded when passenger trains were using the platform so the decision was taken to re-site the station south of Harbour Street in 1895 and this is the building seen above. All traces of the C&W harbour stations were subsequently removed. *AEB5347*

HERNE BAY

62¾ miles from London. Served by frequent express trains from London Victoria and Charing Cross. Journey time 1 hour 40 minutes.

Herne Bay has been planned to suit many tastes. Its natural attractiveness makes it very suitable for family holidays, but modern entertainment has not been overlooked. Like the rest of Kent it is renowned for its crisp, tonic air, its dry climate and favourable record for sunshine. Cinemas, the Grand Pier pavilion, King's Hall Theatre and Ballroom, concerts and dancing all provide indoor entertainment.

Class N1 No. 31879 rounds the curve and runs into the popular holiday and residential destination of Herne Bay on 7 September 1958 with an up service to London Bridge. In the mid 1930s there were over 155,000 tickets issued annually to the resort from London termini and today healthy commuter traffic sustains the frequent electrified services. The large platform end balloon water tanks were a feature of stations on this route but steam age infrastructure was swept away with the electrification scheme of the following year. There was no footbridge here but a subway, seen behind the railings on the right, linked the platforms. All six members of the three cylinder N1 class were based at Hither Green depot at this time before their transfer en bloc to Tonbridge in May the following year. *PH658*

WESTGATE-ON-SEA

72½ miles from London. Served by frequent express trains from London Victoria. Journey time approx. 2 hours.

Westgate-on-Sea, part of the borough of Margate, is a completely self-contained family resort. Behind the *mile long promenade along the sea wall are lawns and gardens. Although it has not the more strenuous attractions which abound in some larger resorts, it has plenty of entertainment. Its comprehensive shopping centre and main line railway station are within a stone's throw of the promenade.*

A rather unkempt "Scotch Arthur" No. 30767 Sir Valence, built by the North British Locomotive Co. in 1925, is seen departing from Westgate-on-Sea on 3 September 1958 with its eight coach train for Ramsgate. This 4-6-0 was originally intended to bear the name "Sir Mordred" but this was changed when Eastleigh realised that in Arthurian legend he was the traitor responsible for the eventual destruction of the Court of King Arthur. It had been based at Stewarts Lane since 1951 but had only ten months left in service before withdrawal in June the following year. On the right Jacksons Garage, over the road from the station, is advertising Regent petrol, perhaps best remembered for its 1960s advertising slogan with the Regent girl in Western costume and the slogans "Get out of town fast!" and "Ride Regent – the lively one!". The brand was subsequently absorbed into Texaco. *PH387*

MARGATE

74 miles from London.

Population 33,500. Aspect North West and North. Climate Bracing. Beach Sand. Early Closing Day Thursday. Attractions – Pier, numerous cinemas, Dreamland Pleasure Park, pavilions, parks (four), *bathing pools (three), Winter Gardens, boating, approach golf (two courses), tennis (hard and grass), bowls, cricket, roller skating and angling. Nine miles of firm tide-washed sands fringe the borough giving safe sea bathing and fun among the rocky pools. Its wonderful health giving air and outstanding sunshine record testify to nature's generous contribution to this pleasant spot.*

No. 21C154 "Lord Beaverbrook" coasts into Margate proudly displaying the "Thanet Belle" headboard and with a smartly turned out set of Pullman coaches, usually numbering ten cars, behind. New to traffic in January 1947 and allocated to Stewarts Lane shed, it was named by Lord Beaverbrook at a ceremony at Waterloo on 16 September 1947. Reallocated to Salisbury in January 1949 it was renumbered to 34054 a couple of months later. "The Thanet Belle" had started life on 31 May 1948 running in the summer months until it changed its name to the "Kentish Belle" in 1951. Thus this undated view was probably taken sometime in the summer of 1948. *(BRL) 648*

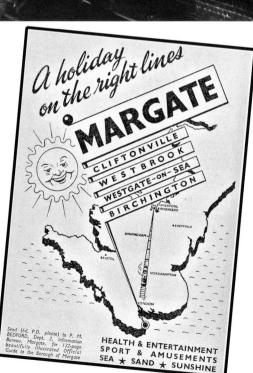

Opposite: Schools Class No. 30928 "Stowe" enters Margate station's curving 520 foot long Platform 1 with a service from London to Ramsgate carrying reporting No. 56. A common feature of major stations is also evident on Platform 1 in the shape of the traditional W H Smith kiosk. The impressive shape of the Booking Hall looms behind the locomotive and there were four through platforms provided together with a westward facing bay on the up side. Canopies on both platforms were flat-roofed in design although that on the down side, seen here on the right, was attached to the main building and incorporated a line of glazed vaulted sections. Conductor rails are in place so this undated view probably dates from the 1958/59 period prior to electrification. No. 30928, carrying a 73B shedplate, was allocated to Bricklayers Arms shed from March 1951 remaining there until October 1961 when it transferred to Brighton for a year until withdrawal in the middle of November 1962. The locomotive was ultimately preserved along with two other members of this very successful Maunsell design. *HW039*

Above: On the 28 March 1959 Standard Class 2 2-6-2T No. 84028 draws the stock of an earlier arrival, consisting of 3 coach Maunsell set No. 230, out of Margate's main platforms prior to setting back into the bay platform seen on the right. The new platform extension in preparation for the twelve car EMU sets is readily apparent as is the new signal gantry ready for the installation of colour light signals which will replace the semaphores seen behind. There appears to have been some sleeper replacement under the track seen in the foreground. No. 84028 had been based at nearby Ramsgate shed since delivery in May 1957 and it was to be withdrawn after a ridiculously short working life of just 8½ years in December 1965. *RCR13086*

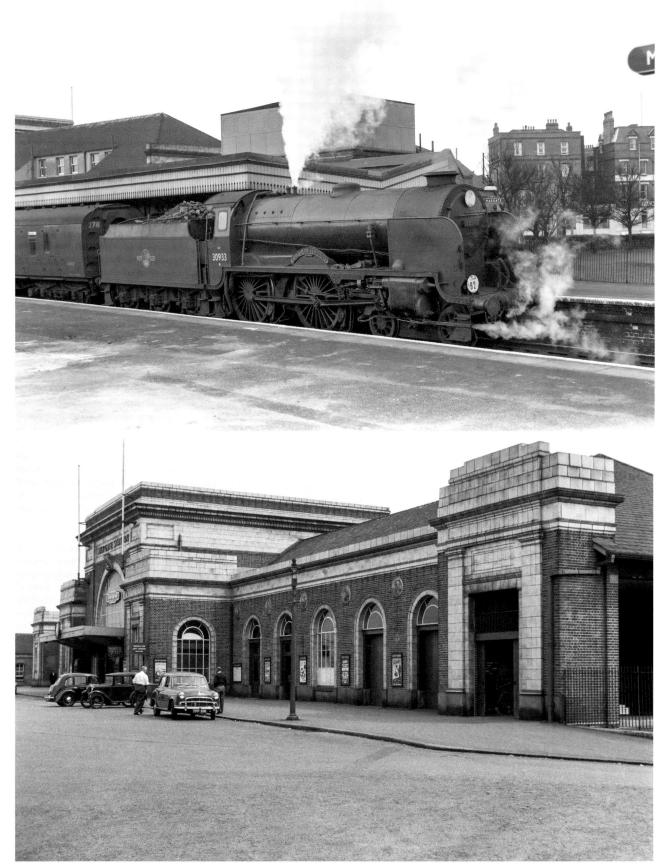

BROADSTAIRS

77¼ miles from London. Served by frequent express trains from London Victoria and Charing Cross. Journey time approx. two hours.

In these hectic modern times it is pleasing to find a seaside resort whose attractions are of the less clamant type and where garishness would be unthinkable. Not that Broadstairs lags behind – far from it. Broadstairs has a grandstand view of shipping linking the world with London and at night, the lightships and other illuminated safeguards against the famous Goodwin Sands are clearly visible. No description of Broadstairs would be complete without reference to Charles Dickens who came to the town in 1837 and stayed at Bleak House overlooking Viking Bay. Broadstairs has had its share of royal patronage. There is no record of the first Elizabeth having slept there but its visitors' list includes both Queen Caroline and Queen Victoria.

Opposite top: Also taken on the 28 March 1959 is this view of Schools No. 30933 "King's Canterbury" seen with steam to spare awaiting departure for Ramsgate and Dover which included coach set No. 278. No. 30933 was another Bricklayers Arms locomotive and there were hopes that it would be preserved after withdrawal from service in 1961. The *Railway Observer* magazine for March 1961 noted that it, along with two other Schools, Nos. 30919 and 30932, were languishing on the scrap road at Ashford Works devoid of nameplates. There was a rumour, unfounded as it turned out, that Canterbury Corporation were interested in purchasing the 4-4-0 but the locomotive met its fate at Ashford Works, being scrapped in December 1961. However, all was not quite lost as one of the nameplates is held by the school in question whilst the other sold at auction in May 2015 for £18,400. *RCR13079*

Opposite bottom: The impressive exterior of Margate station, dating from the 1926 rebuilding, gave the town a spacious new structure capable of handling the vast holiday crowds which poured into the resort in the summer months. The "Margate Station" logo above the front arch formerly read "Southern Railway" but this was replaced upon nationalisation whilst the sausage sign below reads "Southern". The style of the station can best be described as "monumental neo-classical" and is executed in brown brick with stone dressing and a tiled hipped roof. The Booking Hall was constructed in an elliptical shape with pendant lighting. The design was undertaken by the SR's chief assistant modernist architect Maxwell Fry and in 1987 it was awarded Grade II listed status. Fry was also responsible for the design of the new Ramsgate and Dumpton Park stations. The two gentlemen on the forecourt have seemingly just got out of their classic Morris Oxford Series II in this undated 1950s view. *HW311*

Above: In this undated pre-nationalisation image Bulleid pacific No. 21C130 "Watersmeet" enters Broadstairs with a down service to Dover passing the signal box which was to remain in service until July 1959 when it was downgraded to a ground frame. The long sweeping sixty chain curve seen above brought the line as near to the sea as possible. No. 21C130 had entered service in May 1946 and after an initial brief allocation to Ramsgate when new was transferred to Stewarts Lane where it remained until December 1948 after which it moved to Exmouth Junction. This enables us to date this view to the months between the middle of 1946 and renumbering to No. 34030 which took place on 20 November 1948. Although the details recorded with this image state that the train was the "Thanet Belle", given the absence of Pullman cars and the fact that there are only four carriages this is considered to be unlikely. *G3-5*

Almost at journey's end, West Country pacific No. 34017 "Ilfracombe" restarts the 1.08pm service from Charing Cross to Margate from Broadstairs on the 3 September 1958. Although no headboard was carried on this occasion this buffet car service was the "Man of Kent" running via Ashford, Folkestone, Dover and arriving at Margate at 4.05 pm. No. 34017 was one of nine light pacifics based at Ramsgate shed at this time, all being transferred away in May 1959 shortly before the shed closed. *PH421*

THE FINEST AIR IN THE SOUTH

BROADSTAIRS

ON THE KENT COAST

SAFE BATHING
SPORTS FACILITIES
SANDS BEYOND COMPARE
SUITABLE FOR THE FAMILY
SUNSHINE AND SEA
SEVEN DELIGHTFUL BAYS

ENTERTAINMENTS FOR YOUNG AND OLD

Official Guide (6d.) from Entertainments Manager,
Dept. B.R., Garden-on-the-Sands, Broadstairs

RAMSGATE

79½ miles from London. Served by frequent express trains from London Victoria. Journey time 2¼ hours. Refreshment Car on certain trains, also served by the all Pullman "Kentish Belle" and direct through trains from the Midlands.

History records that Hengist and Horsa in AD 449 landed at Ebbsfleet near the part of Ramsgate known as Cliffsend. Messrs. H. & H. may not have known how wise they were in their choice, but thousands and thousands since their time have made no mistake. They keep on coming to Ramsgate and for very good reasons. Ramsgate, one of the most popular of our southern resorts, is proud of its sunshine record which is well above average. Kent is the Garden of England and at Ramsgate its beauty comes down to the sea. So many come again and again and small wonder for this most versatile of resorts has so much to offer – good air, good bathing, good company, good entertainment and, therefore, good fun.

Against a backdrop of Ramsgate's huge brick built station, as rebuilt by the Southern Railway in the 1920s, with its lofty booking hall seen on the far right of this view, Schools Class No. 30915 "Brighton" departs on Monday 6 April 1953 on one of those locomotive duties known as "rounders" which involved a circular route from Victoria via Faversham, Margate, Ramsgate, Dover and Ashford back to Charing Cross or vice versa. In the 1920s a number of significant rationalisations and improvements in the Thanet area had made it possible for a number of trains to and from London to work right around Kent with one crew on this 178 mile circuit. Although the fitting of the Lemaitre exhaust, as seen here, did improve steaming on poorer coal, Bulleid apparently admitted that coal consumption on those Schools which retained their original Maunsell chimney and exhaust was marginally better than that achieved with the Lemaitre system. Ramsgate's six road dead end shed with the east light pattern roof dating from 1930 is seen on the left. This closed to steam in June 1959 when it was converted for EMU use. *RCR4469*

Above: Nearing the end of its working life of nearly 60 years Wainwright C Class No. 31245 engages in shunting empty stock consisting of Maunsell carriage set No. 950 on 28 March 1959. A short dock platform is visible behind the loading gauge and the sidings on the far right are laid on what was once the route of the former line to Ramsgate Town station which closed in 1926 upon rationalisation of lines in the Thanet area. No. 31245 was based locally at Ramsgate shed from where it was transferred to Nine Elms in May 1959 only to be withdrawn a few weeks later. *RCR13073*

Opposite top: Standard Class 5 4-6-0 No. 73083, which would be named "Pendragon" in October 1959, draws the empty stock of the 8.35 am service from Victoria out of Ramsgate on 28 March 1959. This train, which had called at Bromley South, Chatham, Whitstable, Herne Bay and then all stations to Ramsgate, was due in at 10.56 am. Other locomotives in view in this image are West Country No. 34005 "Barnstaple" and, running light engine en route to shed, Class D1 4-4-0 No. 31743. *RCR13065*

Opposite bottom: Passing the four road carriage shed seen on the left, a service for Sandwich, Deal and Dover heads out of Ramsgate on 28 March 1959 powered by West Country class No. 34005 "Barnstaple". It had been the original intention that the Battle of Britain locomotives should serve in the south east of England rather than those pacifics named after West Country locations. Although the majority, but not all, of the Battle of Britain class were initially allocated to the south eastern division, transfers over the years meant that members of the West Country class were often to be seen in the area and by the same token many of the Battle of Britain class migrated to the central and south west divisions. No. 34005, although allocated to Exmouth Junction when new, was transferred to Stewarts Lane in June 1957 before moving to Bricklayers Arms in 1958 staying there until February 1961 when it was reallocated to Salisbury. *RCR13068*

Opposite top: In the months before the Kent Coast Electrification, Stage 1 of which was due for completion by June 1959, crew training trips were undertaken to prepare staff for the new services. Stage 1 of the scheme encompassed extension of the third rail from Gillingham to Faversham, including the Sheerness-on-Sea branch, thence to Dover Marine and Ramsgate. Wainwright H Class tank locomotives were often the motive power chosen for these training trips and No. 31512 of this class is seen at Ramsgate, where the third rail can be seen in place, on 20 March 1959 coupled to an inspection saloon numbered DS1. This was an ex LSWR directors' saloon dating from 1885. It was replaced in 1962 with a newer vehicle and sadly withdrawn in April 1963. Steam did not have a monopoly on these training runs however as the Sulzer Derby Type 2 diesels loaned from the London Midland Region were also noted with this inspection saloon in tow. Motormen for the new EMU service were trained at Stewarts Lane where a new instruction school was opened in November 1958.Training classes comprised twelve drivers, all of whom had previously passed as a driver or fireman on steam locomotives. The course lasted for three weeks, the final week of which consisted of practical instruction including a couple of trips each day.. *RCR13047A*

Opposite bottom: Standard Class 2MT No. 84029 leaves Ramsgate on Saturday 14 May 1960 with a local service, consisting of Maunsell coach set 230 plus van, from Margate to Ashford via Canterbury West. This was an attractive route along the valley of the River Stour even allowing for the blot on the landscape of Chislet Colliery some five miles north east of Canterbury. There were three unadvertised miners' trains from Margate to the colliery daily. The colliery ceased production in 1969, the closure precipitated by the reduction in demand for steam coal following the end of BR steam the previous year. Ten of these 2-6-2Ts were allocated to Ashford at this time for working secondary passenger and freight turns. Half of them left in January 1961 with the remainder following on four months later. No. 84029, after transfer from Ashford to Eastleigh, found its way to a variety of Midland Region sheds ending up at Leicester Midland from where it was withdrawn in June 1964. *RCR14746*

Above: A further view of the locomotive seen on the front cover of this volume, No. 34089 "602 Squadron" at Ramsgate on 2 February 1952, gives us a wider prospect of the station and its immediate environs. Ramsgate was a major centre for passenger rather than freight traffic, deriving its significance not only from the huge volume of summer holiday and excursion traffic but also, after the rationalisation of railways in the area during the 1920s, from the major locomotive servicing facilities which were concentrated here. The main building of the new station provided in the mid 1920s and now Grade II listed can be seen on the far right set at forty-five degrees to the main running lines. Its main drawback was the fact that it was unfortunately at some distance from the sea and the old town centre. Two long curving island platforms were provided at which trains could arrive or depart for London in either direction. Local traffic was also handled and the coaches of the many day excursions were serviced here during their stay on the coast. The signal box seen on the left in front of the carriage cleaning shed controlled the entire layout and was a 50 foot long brick built structure dating from 1926 and designated SR Type 11a. Mechanical signalling was replaced with colour lights in July 1959 upon electrification. *RCR4349*

Opposite top: One of the many less glamorous jobs required when servicing steam locomotives is well illustrated here as the smokebox is cleared of ash by the fireman of D1 Class No. 31735 at Ramsgate shed on 28 March 1959. This locomotive was based at Bricklayers Arms shed at this time and these Maunsell rebuilds of Wainwright's original D class, along with similar Class E1s, had been frequent performers on services from London to Kent for many years. However, their days were numbered with the pending Stage 1 of the Kent Coast Electrification scheme and this example would be transferred to Nine Elms a few weeks after this view was taken. It then moved after a short stay of just a couple of months at 70A to Eastleigh but little work could be found for such elderly 4-4-0s such as those ousted from Kent as more modern steam power was readily available. It lingered on until withdrawal in April 1961. *RCR13069*

Opposite bottom: With the lofty ferro-concrete mechanical coaling plant provided by the Southern Railway for Ramsgate depot as a backdrop, King Arthur Class No.30805 "Sir Constantine" and Schools Class No. 30931 "King's Wimbledon" are seen in the shed yard on 6 April 1953. The tenders of both locomotives look pretty full so have probably just been topped up and, indeed, a footplate crew member can be seen on the tender of the 4-4-0 trimming the coal. The N15 was one of the Eastleigh built Arthurs dating from 1927 and was based at Ashford whilst the V was a Bricklayers Arms locomotive at this time. *RCR4464*

Above: Also seen in Ramsgate shed yard, but this time on 2 February 1952, is Q1 class No. 33024 in very respectable external condition ahead of an unidentified Bulleid pacific which is about to move forward under the coaling plant. Although nearby Tonbridge shed had a number of these austerity 0-6-0s on their books, in fact ten at this time, this particular example was not one of them, being based some considerable distance away at Eastleigh in 1952. It would however be transferred to Tonbridge in October the following year and would last in service until August 1963. Ramsgate shed would briefly gain three of the Q1 class amongst its allocation the following year although all were transferred away after a few months, never to return. *RCR4351*

SANDWICH

90¾ miles from London. Served by frequent express trains from Charing Cross. Also served by the "Man of Kent" from Charing Cross and direct through express trains from the Midlands.

Sandwich, one of the old Cinque Ports, pulsates with historical associations. The sea has receded a mile or so since Sandwich's heyday as a port, but there are many eloquent reminders of its long record. Flourishing light industries indicate that Sandwich is still pulling its weight. In AD 43 the Romans landed at Richborough and the walls of the castle, 1½ miles from Sandwich, are some of the finest examples of Roman masonry still existing in Britain.

Looking east, Schools Class No. 30928 "Stowe" enters Sandwich's platform No. 2 on an unrecorded day in September 1958 with a service from Ramsgate to Dover. No. 30928 was a Bricklayers Arms locomotive from 1949 until October 1961. It went on to become one of the trio of these Maunsell 4-4-0s that survived into preservation, being currently based on the Bluebell Railway. It has a lasting claim to fame in that it was clocked achieving a top speed of 95 mph in 1938, apparently a record for the class. *PH367*

DEAL

86¾ miles from London. Served by frequent express trains from Charing Cross with journey time of approx. 2½ hours.

Deal is famous as a rendezvous for recuperation and convalescence, having its full quota of bracing air which has inspired many an artist, commercial and otherwise, and contributed so much to the reinvigoration of so many less picturesque personalities. There are no musty holes, no cobwebby corners. Vigour pours in with every breath. This was a grand place for family holidays in olden days when bathing machines and so forth were de rigueur. How much more so today, when so many old time restrictions have been confined to the W.P.B.!

Opposite top: Fairburn 2-6-4T No. 42098 enters Deal station on 6 September 1958 with a four coach service sporting a headcode which indicates a train from Ashford to Dover via Minster. A number of these LMR tank locomotives had been built at Brighton Works in 1950/1. After spending time allocated initially to Tunbridge Wells West shed and then Ashford it was transferred to the LMR at Watford. It was withdrawn from service from Carlisle Canal shed in February 1963. Of the 277 members of the class that were constructed, 41 were built at Brighton for use on the SR to replace earlier designs. Seven of these were later transferred to the NE Region between 1952-4 and the remainder to the LMR at the end of 1959 in exchange for BR Standard Class 4 2-6-4Ts that were becoming available. *PH000029*

WALMER

84¾ miles from London Charing Cross with journey time of approx. 2½ hours. Also served by the "Man of Kent" from Charing Cross and direct through express trains from the Midlands.

Walmer and Deal, now united in one borough and thus entitled to dual nomenclature, share in the happy blending of the progressive outlook and the inevitable history and traditions inseparable from this part of England. At high tide swimmers can dive straight from the shelving beach into clear water. At low tide bathing is safe for everyone, including children. The climate is bracing and pleasant. Walmer Castle is the official residence of the Lord Warden of the Cinque Ports, the present Lord Warden being Sir Winston Churchill K.G., O.M., C.H.

Platform and footplate staff exchange greetings as Standard tank No. 80011 coasts in to Walmer in September 1958 whilst a couple of well dressed ladies await its arrival. The carriages carry roof boards which indicate that this was the through service from Birkenhead which ran via Reading, Redhill and Dover terminating at Sandwich. This train was very popular during the summer months although requiring a certain degree of stamina with the prospect of a nine hour journey from Merseyside to Walmer. No. 80011 had emerged from Brighton Works seven years previously and would last in service until the end of SR steam in July 1967. *PH000314*

DOVER

77¼ miles from London Charing Cross and Victoria.

Dover lies in a bay flanked by the famous White Cliffs which have inspired many a poet as well as forming the first view of land to many a visitor from abroad. Dover's streets have fine shops, side by side with *many ancient buildings. It is forgetting the shells and the bombs and caters for the holidaymaker at prices more moderate than most. So much here costs so little. Magnificent cliffs, fine marine walks, historic buildings, beautiful open spaces and the lovely countryside do not make exorbitant demands on the pocket. And there is always the thrill of welcoming the latest Channel swimmer!*

Above: Dover Priory station, named after a local religious establishment, witnesses an unusual visitor from Norwood Junction shed in the shape of Maunsell Q Class No. 30534 on 23 May 1959. Apart from visits to Ashford Works these 0-6-0s were not commonly seen in the South East division and when used on anything other than short passenger workings were certainly not appreciated by footplatemen for their hauling capabilities as they were much more suited to freight duties. The locomotive had been photographed earlier in the day on Dover shed and is seen here at Priory station with a Victoria service via Tonbridge although something seems to be giving the crew cause for concern, possibly a lubrication problem. This view ably demonstrates the situation of the station with the steep chalk escarpment of Dover's Western Heights forming a spectacular backdrop. *AEB4811*

Opposite top: This footplate view was taken from D1 Class No. 31489 on Saturday 14 May 1960 looking north from Dover Priory through the 158 yard long Priory tunnel. Rail access was by twin track tunnels through the chalk both to the north and south of the station. No. 31489 was one of the final trio of these Maunsell rebuilds to be withdrawn in November 1961. The photographer, Dick Riley, had been fortunate enough to enjoy a cab ride from London Bridge, departing at 7.24am to Dover via Orpington, Sevenoaks, Ashford and Folkestone and he would remain on the footplate until the train reached its final stop in Ramsgate hopefully on schedule at 10.30am. *RCR14730*

Opposite bottom: West Country 4-6-2 No. 34013 "Okehampton", with a good head of steam, has charge of an arrival from London via Ashford on 23rd. May 1959 standing at Dover Priory's No. 2 platform. No. 34013 had been rebuilt in October 1957 having run 559,411 miles from new in 1945. It would go on to last in service until the end of SR steam in July 1967 totting up a final mileage of 944,928. At the time of this view it had recently entered workshops for a Light Intermediate overhaul and had received a speedometer and AWS equipment. It was based at Bricklayers Arms shed where it remained until July 1962. Priory station was rebuilt by the Southern Railway in 1932 on the site of the old LC&DR station dating from 1861.The goods yard was on the right and was later used as carriage sidings as seen here. *AEB4810*

Opposite top: Battle of Britain pacific No. 34085 "501 Squadron" has charge of the up "Golden Arrow" on 23 May 1959 and is seen here passing Archcliffe Junction signal box on the left and Dover shed on the right where Class D1 No. 31505 is parked next to an open wooden bodied wagon. The former Archcliffe Junction staff halt is seen in front of the signal box utilising part of the platform of the former Dover Town station which had closed to passengers back in 1914. The "Arrow" was scheduled to leave Dover's Marine station at 5.13pm, assuming the boat from Calais was on time, and was due into Victoria at 6.45pm. The D1 4-4-0 was based at Faversham (73E) at this period but the following month this shed would close and No. 31505 would be transferred to Nine Elms, lasting in traffic until withdrawal in September 1961. *RCR13393*

Opposite bottom: Dover shed is viewed from a passing train on 23 May 1959. The shed seen here was opened by the Southern Railway in 1928 replacing the older shed at Priory and had all the usual facilities including a water softener and 65 ft. turntable. The coaling stage is on the left of this view, access for coal wagons being by means of the concrete ramp. It was constructed on land

reclaimed from the sea and was very exposed to the elements. On show is a variety of stock including a Class O1 0-6-0, an unmodified Bulleid pacific, a diesel shunter and a couple of carriages of birdcage stock. The shed closed in June 1961 and was subsequently demolished. Dominating the background is the dramatic outline of Shakespeare Cliff. *RCR13395*

Above: O1 Class No. 31434 is engaged in shunting on 4 April 1959, the locomotive being on one of the two roads numbered 1 and 2 which ran between the left hand arch of the impressive Dover Marine station and the dockside cranes. The station had only recently re-opened after a week's closure at the end of February during which the platforms had been lengthened in preparation for electrification. Dover shed had the last five of these rebuilds of Stirling's original O Class on their books at this time although this example, along with classmate 31425, would be withdrawn just four months later. One of the others went in May 1959 leaving just two to soldier on until 1961 after which the last in service, No. 31065, was fortunately preserved and today can be found on the Bluebell Railway. The outside springs on the tenders of these 0-6-0s gave these veterans a very Victorian appearance. *RCR13124*

FOLKESTONE

70 miles from London and served by frequent express trains from Charing Cross with refreshment car on certain trains. Journey time approx. 1¾ hours. Also served by the "Man of Kent" from Charing Cross and direct through trains from the Midlands.

Folkestone is a thoroughly modern resort equipped with abundant facilities for fun and games. Stately

cliffs, sheltered undercliffs, spacious parks and gracious gardens and a sea front stretching for about 5 miles from the famous Warren in the east to Sandgate in the west and at the back the noble sweep of the North Downs all bear lavish testimony to nature's prodigality. Among the many attractions is The Leas, a famous cliff top promenade of lawns and flower beds from which the coastline of France is clearly visible in good weather. Day trips to France during the summer are now very popular.

Above: Battle of Britain pacific No. 34085 "501 Squadron", carrying full regalia and attracting the attention of two small boys on the end of the platform, arrives at Folkestone Junction with the premier train of the line, the "Golden Arrow", on 25 October 1958. This Pullman service left London's Victoria station at 1pm and was due into Folkestone at 2.38pm. Waiting in the wings is R1 tank No. 31128 which, with other helpers, will take the train down the incline to the harbour station once the Bulleid has taken the stock into one of the sidings on the south side of the line. Once the empty stock had been worked up the incline from the harbour it was then taken on to Dover by the main line locomotive, which had been serviced at the junction shed, in readiness for the return trip to London. After their sea crossing and train from Calais Maritime to Paris Nord, passengers would arrive in the French capital at 9.45pm French time. The proximity of the three road shed to the station is apparent with an unidentified Standard 2-6-0 seen outside. *RCR12933*

Opposite top: On the 14 May 1960 D1 4-4-0 No. 31489 arrives at Folkestone Junction with a service for Ramsgate. On the left Schools Class No. 30918 "Hurstpierpoint" reverses out of the sidings into the up platform road. The D1 still carries an original shedplate for 74D which had formerly been the shed code for Tonbridge; however this had been changed to 73J eighteen months previously in October 1958. Note the insulator pots in situ ready to receive the third rail which would be installed as part of Phase 2 of the Kent Coast electrification scheme going live through Folkestone the following year. *RCR14728*

Opposite bottom: Folkestone Junction shed yard contains standby R1 tanks Nos. 31010 and 31107 whilst the active member of the banking fraternity steams past in the shape of WR pannier tank No. 4616 on 4 April 1959. No. 31010 displays the cut down cab and Urie type short chimney of those locomotives modified to work the former Canterbury & Whitstable line with its low headroom. In January 1959 a dozen WR pannier tanks of Class 57XX were reallocated to the SR, six to Nine Elms where they replaced Drummond M7 tanks and six to Dover where they operated out of the depot's sub-shed at Folkestone Junction. Introduced in 1933 these 5700 Class panniers were used to replace the ageing ex SER R1 tanks on incline banking duties. The initial allocation was Nos. 4601, 4610, 4616, 4626, 4630 and 4631, being joined by a seventh member, No. 3633, in April 1960. *RCR13116*

Above: R1 No. 31337 stands at the head of the next departure from the Harbour station on 19 May 1957. The locomotive crew look on from their cab as a railwayman heads off carrying a white tail lamp. The line leading off to the right, accessed from the up line, led to carriage sidings and had the effect of splitting the up platform into two sections. The down or arrival platform had been lengthened in 1938 and provided with a substantial canopy over much of its length and it also sported a small refreshment kiosk as seen on the left. Following the cessation of the regular cross Channel Seacat service in 2000 the Harbour station then handled only the twice weekly VSOE Pullman tourist services until 2006. It officially closed at the end of May 2014 although the last enthusiast special hauled by 70013 "Oliver Cromwell" had run in March 2009. The station has since been restored as part of the extensive harbour area redevelopment scheme. *AEB2118*

Opposite top: A charming period view taken on 19 July 1957 featuring visitors in their best "casual" gear including sports jackets and caps watching the passage of a boat train being banked up the incline from the Harbour station by R1 tank No. 31107. At the front of the train were two further R1s in the shape of Nos. 31047 and 31128. The schoolboy with his smart blazer and binoculars is perhaps more interested in the availability of "Minerals" from the adjacent snack bar than in the train. The Pent Stream, from which the café takes its name, at one time used to flow under the windows of houses along Tontine Street but today flows in a culvert beneath the street and then under a car park and Chummy's seafood kiosk before emptying into the harbour under what is now known as Gigi's café. *AEB2435*

Opposite bottom: An up service described on the carriage boards as a "Continental Express – Short Sea Route" nears the top of the incline from the Harbour station to Folkestone Junction triple headed by R1 tanks Nos. 31107, 31337 and 31128. The employment of six footplatemen and a guard must have made this one of the most expensive, though short, sections of track to work on the SR. Merchant Navy No. 35015 "Rotterdam Lloyd" was waiting at the junction to take over the service to London on the 25 October 1958. In the winter of 1958 one could leave Paris Nord at 8.12am, arrive at Calais Maritime at 12.15pm, catch the ferry and arrive into Folkestone at 12.45pm (British time - one hour difference) and be deposited at Victoria by 3.05pm. Alternatively one could leave Brussels at 7.04am and, changing at Lille, could arrive at Calais at 11.33am, catch the same ferry and arrive into Folkestone and London at the times above. A 1st. Class Pullman car was provided on this service and a 1st. Class return from Folkestone to Calais would have set you back the princely sum of £13 10/- (£13.50). *RCR12923*

HYTHE

66¾ miles from London and served by frequent express trains from London Charing Cross to Sandling or Folkestone Central, thence by bus.

Hythe is an ancient Cinque Port deserted by the sea. Its ancient harbour is silted up but in every other respect Hythe is a perfectly up to date and sizeable

resort. Its seafront, half a mile away, stretches for about two miles. The beach is of shingle with sand at low tide and perfectly safe for bathing. It is particularly proud of its Royal Military canal, dating from the Napoleonic Wars, and Hythe's greatest annual event, the Venetian Fete, one of England's greatest water carnivals, is held on the canal. (NB: This still operates today on a biennial basis.)

Opposite: On the 25 October 1958 Merchant Navy No. 35015 "Rotterdam Lloyd" sets off for London having collected its boat train from the sidings on the south of the main line, the stock of which had been previously hauled up from the Harbour station. This pacific was the only rebuilt example to work on the south eastern section of the SR; the other examples, Nos. 35001 and 35028, based at Stewarts Lane at this time, being in original air smoothed form for the duration of their stay at 73A. No. 35015 was rebuilt at Eastleigh in June 1958 and surprisingly was returned to Stewarts Lane until the Kent Coast electrification caused the trio to be moved away to Nine Elms in May 1959. The ornate water crane seen on the far left is particularly noteworthy. *RCR12926*

Above: The decrepit state of Hythe station is testament to the fact that the branch line had little time left to run, closing just four months after the date of this view. The remains of the bomb damaged former Parcels Office seen to the right of the locomotive also does nothing to enhance the scene. Having run round its two coach train, consisting of push pull set No. 721, Class H tank No. 31521 is ready to return to the main line at Sandling Junction on 25 August 1951. Hythe station was inconveniently sited high above the town and became the terminus of the branch following closure of the section onwards to Sandgate in 1931. This truncation rendered the branch without watering facilities so a water tower and crane were provided as seen here at the north end of the up platform at Hythe. It would appear from the water emanating from the bag that the locomotive has just replenished its tanks. *RCR4289*

NEW ROMNEY & LITTLESTONE-ON-SEA

78 miles from London. Served by frequent express trains to Ashford thence by branch line train to New Romney.

Romney Marsh is an area of quiet charm, with many attractions for the nature lover. Its principal claim to

fame is that it grows more sheep to the acre than any other part of England. New Romney has been left high and dry by the capricious sea. The narrow gauge Romney, Hythe and Dymchurch Railway plays an important part in the life of these little coast towns.

Opposite top: Having previously deposited its train at the platform No. 31521 engages in some light shunting in the grass grown goods yard on 25 August 1951. The yard contained a 30 cwt crane seen on the far right where a coal yard was also located. The sidings on the left had already been lifted by this date and in spite of having closed back in 1931 the platform mounted signal box still survived twenty years later. When closure proposals for the passenger service were announced it was the original intention to continue to handle goods traffic at Hythe, the principal inbound freight being coal and stores for a local brewery with outbound goods consisting mainly of parcels traffic and empties from the brewery. However, with anticipated costs of £8,500 required in the near future according to the Civil Engineer's Department it was decided that this expense could not be justified and the line closed completely. *RCR4284*

Opposite bottom: Nearly three years after closure this was the desolate picture at Hythe on 19 October 1954 when only the platforms of the former station remained. Similar scenes would be repeated many times all over the country in the coming years particularly after the Beeching cuts of the early 1960s. Housing now occupies the site and trains to Hythe bringing holidaymakers to this part of the Kent coast are but a distant memory. However, tourists and locals alike can still experience train travel from Hythe albeit on the narrow gauge Romney, Hythe and Dymchurch Railway (RH&DR) which has its eastern terminus in the town. *RCR5582*

Above: H Class No. 31307 stands ready for departure at New Romney & Littlestone-on-Sea with the 3.04pm service for all stations to Ashford on 15 August 1960. Some services on the branch only went as far as the junction with the Hastings-Ashford line at Appledore but several, including this one, continued through to Ashford, a journey of 22 miles which took 48 minutes. This Wainwright 0-4-4T was, as might be expected, based at Ashford, where it had been constructed in 1906, and from where it would be withdrawn twelve months later after a working life of 54 years. The station had been provided with two platforms but only the one seen here was generally used as the grass grown platform on the far right testifies. *W54920*

WINCHELSEA

71½ miles from London. Served by express trains from Charing Cross with change of train at Ashford. Journey time approx. 2 ¼ hours.

An ancient town with Cinque port privileges, the Winchelsea we know today took the place of an older

Winchelsea engulfed by the sea in the 13th.c. It still remains a remarkable example of town planning. A small beach town has sprung up on Winchelsea beach, now made safe from the sea's encroachments. It is a pleasant little resort with good bathing facilities.

Opposite top: Standard tank No. 84029 has charge of the branch service on 16 August 1959 hauling 3-coach BR Mk1. set No. 529. The level of passenger service was improved following the replacement of steam by two car DEMUs in 1962 providing 11 trains a day, most of which ran through to Ashford. However this was insufficient to save the passenger service which was duly withdrawn in 1967. No. 84029 was a recent transferee to Ashford where it would remain until May 1961. *JB206*

Opposite bottom: DEMU No. 1120 waits at New Romney in 1964 with a service for Ashford. The level crossing gates seen in the background mark the site of a single line extension which was laid in 1927 to an exchange siding with the adjacent RH&DR station on the opposite side of Station Road, this being used to facilitate coal deliveries to that steam powered railway. Unit No. 1120 was one of the second batch of two car units, designated 2H, built in 1958. They were specifically constructed for services on the Hastings to Ashford and New Romney lines where two cars were considered to be sufficient. They remained as two car sets until 1979 when they were strengthened to three cars and re-designated Class 205. No. 1120 remained in service until September 1987. *NS200957*

Above: A service from Hastings enters one of the staggered platforms at Winchelsea on 21 September 1950 with a service for Ashford drawn by St. Leonards depot based C Class No.31037. The crossing keeper's house can be seen on the left adjacent to the level crossing which was situated just beyond the up platform. The main station house can be seen behind the coaches on the right of this view. The station was in a rather isolated position some distance from the village which had to be accessed down an unlit and winding country lane and therefore probably attracted few tourists other than walkers. The former up platform seen here is the only one in existence today now that the route has been largely singled. *RCR4195*

HASTINGS

62½ miles from London. Served by frequent trains from London Charing Cross and Victoria. Journey time approx. 2 hours.

In summer the Channel breezes ensure a constant supply of bracing, tonic air. Hastings is proud of its spacious seafront with its double promenade and covered walk, its sun-trap shelters and luxurious sun lounge, where light music and refreshments are available. No visitor need ever spend a dull moment.

The White Rock Pavilion houses a famous concert party in summer and the Municipal Orchestra and famous visiting orchestras in winter. Hastings Pier is replete with seaside amusements. The well known medical baths offer numerous treatments for rheumatism and allied disorders at moderate cost. Old Hastings itself, quite distinct from the modern resort, lies in a narrow valley opening onto a shingly shore. Sturdy sailing boats drawn up on the shore add much warm colour to the scene which is a favourite rendezvous for artists.

Above: Star performers on the Charing Cross – Hastings route in steam days were the Maunsell Schools class which, following the lifting of weight and gauging restrictions, were cleared for use on the line in 1931. These 4-4-0s were specifically designed for the tight tunnel clearances and steep gradients of the line and No. 30921 "Shrewsbury" is seen having arrived at Hastings with a train from London, the first coach of which is an SECR birdcage brake, on 16 July 1950. No. 921 had been renumbered to 30921 just 4 months before the date of this view and given BR black livery adorned with the "cycling lion" emblem on its tender. It was to go through several livery changes in its lifetime including malachite green (twice), olive green, BR black (twice) and finally BR green until withdrawal in December 1962. The line from Brighton through Hastings to the next station at Ore, where there was space to accommodate a new electric depot, had been electrified in 1935 hence the presence of the third rail. *RCR4092*

Opposite top: Also at the eastern end of Hastings station in a similar position to the previous image is Wainwright C class 0-6-0 No. 31038 seen on 20 September 1950 reversing out of the station tender first under clear signals. Although adorned with "British Railways" on the tender and its new number, in the 30XXX sequence allocated to the SR, on the cabside it does not carry a smokebox numberplate but the bufferbeam does display its new identity. This was a recent reallocation to St. Leonards depot where it stayed until June 1952 when it moved to Tonbridge, staying there until withdrawal in March 1954 having been in service for a little over 52 years. These were primarily freight locomotives but could be seen on secondary passenger services across the south east including the famous Hop Pickers' specials. Remarkably one of the class, No. 31271 which, along with two other examples, had passed into departmental service in 1963 as DS240, could claim to be the last locomotive to raise steam on the SR when it was used as a stationary boiler in Kimberley Sidings at Ashford to steam clean axle bearings. This duty did not finish until August 1967, a month after the official end of steam on the SR. *Brian Hilton*

Opposite bottom: The headcode carried by Class U1 No. 31896 on 16 July 1950 indicates that this was a recently arrived service from London via Redhill, Haywards Heath, Lewes and Eastbourne where reversal was required. This was a Redhill based locomotive at this date and one of 21 members of this class of 3 cylinder Maunsell moguls. Hastings was well served by two direct routes from London, that via Tonbridge and Tunbridge Wells Central, and the longer route via Redhill, Lewes and Eastbourne. One could also arrive from the east via Ashford, changing to a connecting service to Hastings. Passengers from further afield could reach Hastings on a through express from Chester serving Shrewsbury, Birmingham, Oxford and Reading. *RCR4094*

ST. LEONARDS

61¾ miles from London. Served by frequent trains from Charing Cross and Victoria.

Sheltered by gently rising hills, winter here is usually mild with plenty of sunshine and St. Leonards is *generally free from fog. Numerous parks and gardens include St. Leonards Gardens and the town is well equipped with shops, restaurants and cafes with plentiful hotel and boarding house accommodation available.*

Above: The up platform of St. Leonards West Marina station is just visible on the far right of this view and provided a grandstand view of the adjacent shed coded 74E. On shed on 26 August 1956 are Schools Class No. 30908 "Westminster", A1X No. 32678 and behind the terrier N Class No. 31828. By the following year the shed's role was much diminished with the introduction of the Hastings diesel scheme. The shed here effectively closed in June 1958 although locomotives continued to be stabled and serviced here until November 1967. No. 30908 was transferred to Stewarts Lane in May 1957 with No. 32678 going to Fratton in May 1958 for use on the Hayling Island branch. West Marina station itself was to close in July 1967 being rather inconveniently sited and given that there were two other stations, West St. Leonards and Warrior Square, serving the town.. *AEB1697*

Opposite top: The down side platform of West Marina station seen on the right provided an even better view of the shed, a panorama also "enjoyed" by the residents of the houses perched on top of the chalk face created by excavation for the shed yard. Not much evidence of washing hanging on lines in the gardens of these houses but that was perhaps understandable! Parked up out of steam on 26 August 1956 were R1 tank No. 31174, A1X No. 32670, H Class No. 31269 and an unidentified Schools Class. The shed, which had three through and one dead end road, was rebuilt by the SR with a steel and asbestos pitched roof and at the date of this view had an allocation of 15 Schools, 1 C, 7 H, 1 R1, 3 A1X and 2 Q1 class. *AEB1692*

Opposite bottom: On that same August day in 1956 the attractive lines of Class L 4-4-0 No. 31765 grace the shed yard whilst a fireman draws forward coal from the tender of Schools Class No. 30924 "Haileybury" on an adjacent track. No. 31765 was delivered in 1914 being constructed by Beyer, Peacock and was, at the time of this photograph, allocated to Faversham shed along with three other members of the class. *AEB1698*

BEXHILL-ON-SEA

62 miles from London served by frequent Southern Electric express trains from Victoria, also expresses from Charing Cross. Journey time approx. 2 hours.

Today Bexhill is a compact modern resort in which most of the accommodation for visitors is situated along the front so that the sea is never far away. Compact though it is, Bexhill manages to convey a sense of spaciousness. There is plenty of room on its *sandy beaches, on the sports greens and golf courses, and, above all, space to sit and just do nothing at all for as long as one likes. Egerton Park has a pavilion for theatrical and vaudeville productions but the town's piece de resistance is the De La Warr pavilion, a magnificent modern building which contains a restaurant, sun terraces, a roof garden and colonnade, a theatre and conference or concert hall.*

Above: Class D3 0-4-4T No. 32388 waits at Bexhill West terminus with a two coach shuttle service to the main line at Crowhurst, 4½ miles away, on 16 July 1950. The short trains which operated latterly were dwarfed by the scale of platform provision at the terminus. Although the main station building was electrically lit, the platforms, as can be seen here, were lit by gas. Whilst on the subject of gas, it will be seen that parked on the runround road is a gas container wagon normally used for replenishing the gas supply for dining car cookers. In 1926 six first class Pullman kitchen cars were introduced to the Charing Cross - Hastings line by the Southern Railway, the gas containers based at Bexhill West being used to replenish these vehicles. Pullmans remained on the Hastings route until dieselisation in June 1958 and two of them, "Theodora" and "Barbara", were preserved and can be seen today on the K&ESR. The Billinton D3 tanks dating from the 1890s were coming to the end of their working lives at this time with this example being withdrawn in December of the following year and most going by 1953 although one did soldier on until 1955. On the Bexhill West branch they would be replaced by Wainwright H Class tank locomotives until dieselisation came in 1958. *RCR4093*

Opposite top: Although the exterior of Bexhill West, formerly Bexhill-on-Sea at opening and then plain Bexhill, shows it to have been a handsome building, it was something of a poor relation when it came to rail services serving the resort. This was often the case when a latecomer on the railway scene arrived in a town already served by an established route such as occurred with Bexhill which had been served by the LBSCR since 1846. It was not until 1902 that the local railway backed by the SER opened their station in Bexhill. Whilst offering a shorter journey to London it suffered from two disadvantages namely its position in the more underdeveloped western end of the town, which was reinforced when the main station was afforded the suffix "Central" in 1923 whilst the SER station became "West" in 1929, and the inertia it had to overcome in dislodging travellers from their established patterns of travel. Nonetheless it was a lavish building constructed in yellow and red brick with Bath stone dressing. It had a Welsh slate roof adorned with a clock tower. Even with the odd through train and some through coaches from the capital being detached from main line trains at Crowhurst, thus avoiding the need to change trains, passenger traffic never really lived up to expectations and the branch closed in 1964. A fine collection of motor vehicles, including the unmistakeable "teardrop" shape of a Jowett Javelin outside the main entrance, adorn the forecourt at, if the clock is to be believed, 4.35pm on the sunny afternoon of 28 July 1953. The station building now houses a fine restaurant, *RCR4700*

Opposite bottom: Replacements for the D3s came in the form of H Class 0-4-4Ts such as this example, No. 31519, seen here in the expansive though seemingly deserted station on 7th. August 1956 with a two coach push-pull carriage set. There were two island platforms 700 feet in length with only the left hand one having a canopy. Platform 4, out of view on the far right, never received any track and platform 3, which was rarely used after the early years, was, as can be seen, largely covered in grass. No. 31519 was based at nearby St. Leonards shed at this date along with six other members of the class and was withdrawn in February 1961. *AEB1540*

EASTBOURNE

65¾ miles from London. Served by Southern Electric express trains from Victoria and London Bridge. Journey time approx. 1½ hours.

The broad promenade is lined with fine hotels and its famous carpet gardens and quaint fishing station, past the pier, are a constant joy to the eye.

The Redoubt, a 2,500 seat open air theatre, where a special show for children is given every morning, in mid-summer, and the Grand Parade Bandstand Area, where 3,000 people can listen in comfort to famous military bands, are favourite rendezvous. There are sea trips to Beachy Head lighthouse or down the Channel from the pier, or, for the more venturesome, no-passport day trips across the Channel.

Above: A pair of 2 NOL EMUs, led by No. 1820, stand at Eastbourne's terminus station carrying headcode 18 indicating a service to Brighton. These EMUs were introduced in 1934 formed of a motor third brake and a driving trailer composite with no corridors or toilets – hence their designation NOL. The 1935 electrification of the Brighton-Eastbourne-Hastings line and the Seaford and Horsted Keynes branches required a large fleet of EMUs to operate local services. They were also used on Brighton – West Worthing stopping services and 89 units were built in two batches using pre-Grouping LSWR coaches on new underframes. With their wooden bodywork more than half a century old by the mid 1950s, withdrawals of the NOLs began in 1956 with the last survivors going in 1959. The poster on the far right is advertising a visit of controversial Jewish comedian and musician Mickey Katz who specialised in Yiddish humour which was apparently not to everyone's taste. *C481*

Opposite top: An earnest platform conversation seems to be under way between the driver and guard of a "Cuckoo Line" train prior to departure from Eastbourne to Tunbridge Wells West on 10 July 1952. Extremely modern motive power is provided in the shape of Ivatt tank No.41318 which, as can be judged from the pristine condition of the locomotive, had been allocated new to Tunbridge Wells West shed just the previous month along with classmate No. 41319. This pair would be joined by two other examples in September whilst Eastbourne shed played host to Nos. 41316 and 41317 although their stay here would be relatively short, both departing for Tunbridge Wells West in September. No. 41318 was to spend its whole working life, of just over 11 years, on the SR, being withdrawn from Exmouth Junction shed in September 1963. *Ron H Fullager*

Opposite bottom: LMR Fairburn tank No. 42102 waits for departure time at Eastbourne's platform 1 with a service for the "Cuckoo Line" to Tunbridge Wells. This locomotive, a product of Brighton Works, spent some nine years based at Tunbridge Wells West shed from new with a short break from September 1951 to March 1952 spent at Three Bridges. The goods yard on the right contains a reasonable quantity of freight wagons with the substantial goods shed apparent in the background. *C487*

NEWHAVEN

56¼ miles from London. Served by frequent Southern Electric trains from Victoria, in certain cases with change of train at Haywards Heath.

Though small in size, Newhaven performs its important share of linking this country with the outside world by the fine cross-Channel boats on the Newhaven – Dieppe service and by the ships of other nations. The sheltered sands of the Harbour Beach give the children many happy hours and Newhaven is a splendid centre for cliff and countryside rambling.

Opposite top: Eastbourne shed, coded 75G and the third provided for this resort, opened in 1911 and consisted of a seven road brick built through shed with a slated roof. Badly damaged during World War II it was never repaired and the light and airy aspect of the above view was merely a reflection of that fact that the shed had lost its roof covering leaving the iron cross members remaining. Even these were subsequently removed leaving just the outside walls standing. It was closed in 1952 but continued to service visiting traction and was also used to store condemned locomotives awaiting scrapping at Ashford Works. It was abandoned in 1968 and demolished a year later. In this view taken on 14 October 1950, a couple of Class B4X 4-4-0s, Nos. 32043 and 3207?, the last digit being obscured but likely to be 1,2 or 3, all of which were allocated here at this time, are visible together with a Class E5 0-6-2T No.32591. The less than successful B4Xs were demoted to secondary duties after 1929 and all were withdrawn by 1951. *RCR4207*

Opposite bottom: K mogul No. 32348 brings a portion of an inter-regional service into Eastbourne past the platform flower bed and a rather un-PC poster for Robertson's Golden Shred. Carriage boards indicate that this was part of the through service from Chester, Shrewsbury, Birmingham and Reading which split a portion for Hastings via Brighton and Eastbourne at Redhill. The main train conveying through portions for Folkestone, Dover and Sandwich and for Canterbury, Ramsgate and Margate would split further at Ashford. *C549*

Above: Under the watchful gaze of Newhaven Harbour signal box, demolished only recently in 2020, ex LBSCR Class H2 atlantic No. 32426 "St. Alban's Head" waits to depart with an up boat train from Newhaven Harbour (Marine) station on 20 August 1950. The Harbour station opened in May 1886 and was renamed Newhaven Marine in 1984. The lines to the left led to the Seaford terminus of the branch from Lewes. The Marine station, which has a single platform sufficient for 12 coaches, also contains a "Hornby" electric locomotive seen to the right of the Marsh 4-4-2. These atlantics had handled boat trains for a number of years in the 1920s and 1930s and indeed even after electrification in 1935 they continued on such duties after WW2, not being displaced until the mid 1950s. Following reductions in the number of ferry sailings over the years the Marine station was closed to the public in 2006 over safety concerns but continued to be served by a daily "parliamentary train" without passengers until engineering works caused the cancellation of even this in 2019 but it has since been resinstated. Currently DFDS operates a ferry service from Newhaven to Dieppe. *RCR4108*

Opposite top: Moving up the line slightly from the previous image is this shot of Newhaven Harbour station, also taken on 20 August 1950. This station remains open today (just) along with Newhaven Town further up the line towards Lewes. (Newhaven Harbour sees a peak-hour service on weekdays only.) The line from the Harbour station towards Seaford was singled as an economy measure in 1975 and the extensive sidings seen in the foreground here are long gone. *RCR4110*

Opposite bottom: A closer view of Class H2 No. 32426 "St.Alban's Head" heading an up boat train away from Newhaven on 20 August 1950 affords the opportunity to appreciate the graceful lines of these Marsh atlantics. Named after geographical features of the south coast, with the exception of Trevose Head which is in north Cornwall, St. Alban's Head is located three miles south west of Swanage. Based at Brighton's sub shed of Newhaven at the time of nationalisation, all six members of the class were subsequently transferred to Brighton from where the last survivor, "Beachy Head", was withdrawn in 1958, a sad loss to preservation although there is currently a new build "Beachy Head" in progress on the Bluebell Railway. *RCR4109*

Above: On 12 July 1950 Class A1X No.32636 trundles cautiously with its rake of wagons from the West Quay branch over Newhaven's old swing bridge which crossed the River Ouse. Dating from 1866 the bridge was replaced in 1974 by one further upstream. One of the main rail traffics over the bridge was beach shingle and Newhaven shed had a couple of these "Terriers" on its books at this time for handling freight on the numerous dock lines. *RCR4082*

All change at BRIGHTON

BRIGHTON

50½ miles from London. Served by frequent Southern Electric express trains from Victoria and London Bridge. Journey time 1 hour. Also served by the all Pullman "Brighton Belle" from Victoria and direct through trains from the North, Midlands, West of England and South Wales.

Brighton is the focal point of that delectable part of Southern England known as the "Sunny South". Even when, as sometimes happens, the sun is not actually shining, the inhabitants claim that there is a certain "something in the air" which is equally beneficial. The beach is of shingle with sand at low tide and the sea has few currents and no undertow and is thus ideally safe for bathing. From the top of the Devil's Dyke, at the back of the town, one of the finest views in England stretches away northwards across Sussex and westwards towards Hampshire, whilst, on the other side, shimmers the distant sea. But scenery, however beautiful, is not everything. For the active minded, who have not yet reached the deckchair stage, Brighton offers a bewildering catalogue of outdoor sport and amusement. There are two piers, Palace and West, open air band concerts, horse racing, greyhound racing and, in neighbouring Hove, county cricket and Third League football. There are seven theatres, twelve cinemas, four ballrooms, an ice rink, ice shows, the zoo at Withdean, amusement arcades and all the fun of the fair. You cannot be dull in Brighton

In this pre nationalisation image Class E5X No. 2576 departs from Brighton station on 29 June 1946 with the magnificent backdrop of the grade II listed 1882-3 trainshed behind. Such an architectural gem was appropriate for the Southern's premier seaside resort and even as recently as 2018/19 Brighton was considered to be the seventh busiest station in the UK outside London. Four of the E5 class of thirty locomotives, designed by Billinton and built between 1902-4, were rebuilt as class E5X with a larger boiler in 1911 including No. 2576 which was named "Brenchley", a village in the borough of Tunbridge Wells. This example soldiered on for another nine years before withdrawal in 1955, the final members of the class being withdrawn in January 1956. *RCR1268*

The 4.36 pm service to Tunbridge Wells West via Lewes, Uckfield and Eridge erupts from Brighton's penultimate easterly platform No. 9 on 23 June 1951 with I1X Class No. 2002, very much on its last knockings, in charge. The original I1 class 4-4-2Ts designed by Marsh were constructed at Brighton Works in 1906/7 but were found to be poor steamers so Maunsell rebuilt them with larger boilers between 1925-32. No. 2002 seen here, which never received its BR number of 32002, was to last in service only a few days after this view was taken, being withdrawn from its home shed at Brighton the following month thereby rendering the whole class extinct. A "Birdcage" set forms the coaching stock and these elderly vehicles were often to be found on these workings which at this time provided an approximate, if irregular, hourly service to Tunbridge Wells West with some services continuing through the Central station in Tunbridge Wells to terminate at Tonbridge. *RCR4248*

No doubt about the location of this view of K Class mogul No. 32353 seen on the 7 October 1962. The sign on the wall of Brighton Works with its large arrow indicating to travellers that their journey was almost over would no doubt be a relief especially to those holidaymakers who have travelled from the Midlands or even further afield on one of the through holiday services operated from such places as Birkenhead, Sheffield, Manchester and South Wales. No. 32353 was specially "bulled up" to haul the RCTS "Sussex Special" railtour on the leg from Brighton to Preston Park thence via the Cliftonville curve to Shoreham, Steyning, Leatherhead, Epsom and ending at London Bridge. The locomotive is seen crossing Montpelier Junction where the east coast line branched away to the right whilst the London line curved away to the left. As a reversal was required the locomotive operated tender first to Preston Park where it ran round its train after collecting the tour stock which had been brought into Brighton from Newhaven by A1X No. 32636 and E6 No. 32418. *RCR16848*

Opposite top: Generations of railway enthusiasts must have walked up from the station to Howard Place which was situated atop the chalk cliff that was left when the west coast line to Shoreham was carved out of the hillside. For those brave – or foolish – enough to climb up the wall and sit on the fence or even worse to drop down the other side of the wall to perch on the small ledge which had a sheer drop down to the rails below, the reward was the view seen. On 1 July 1951 there was plenty to see on shed with C2X No. 32443 in the foreground sharing the wheel drop with a Fairburn tank and adjacent to a Maunsell mogul. C2X consecutively numbered classmate No. 32442 is in good external condition in front of the water softening tanks which, given that Brighton was situated in chalk country, were very necessary to reduce scaling problems. Behind the massive water tank is the pitched roof of the former carriage shed, which became part of the loco shed following the removal of the carriage works to Lancing. This function ceased in the 1930s and the building was converted into a workshop for use by the Road Motor Engineers Department. Beyond that on the right is the distant London Road viaduct. Brighton shed was closed to steam in June 1964 and demolished in 1966. *RCR4251*

Opposite bottom: A stunning panorama across the rooftops of Brighton taken on 23 August 1952 reveals the architectural gem of the sharply curving London Road Viaduct consisting of 27 arches containing a reported ten million bricks and stretching for a total length of 1,200 feet. This shot has the added bonus of a six coach steam hauled service crossing hauled by what appears to be one of the new Standard tank locomotives which in the early 1950s were beginning to replace older motive power. The viaduct carries the east coast line from Brighton to Lewes and beyond and opened in 1846, affording passengers a bird's eye view of the town. The large arch towards the middle of the picture crosses Preston Road, the main A23 London Road out of the town. When first built the viaduct stood alone in a country setting but development quickly swallowed up the green fields and dense urban housing now covers the foreground and the hills behind. *RCR4366*

Above: Preston Road and its lofty viaduct arch taken on 23 August 1952. The piers of the arch are 22 feet thick at the base and 19½ feet thick at the top and each pier contains a jack arch with a semi-circular soffit. Apart from the main railway feature dominating this view, close study reveals a wealth of detail. One of the shops on the left advertises the fact that furniture was bought and sold and next to the Post Office is an establishment which sold pipes, cigars and where you could have your films developed. Outside the Post Office was a pillar box partly obscured by one of the poles supporting the overhead wires for the trolleybuses which continued to operate in Brighton until June 1961. On the opposite side of the road is a stonemason's emporium next to the assorted secondhand appliances and furniture stacked on the pavement whilst further along is a building advertising Evangelistic Meetings every Sunday at 6:30 pm with Bible study on Wednesdays at 7pm. Advertising hoardings attached to the viaduct extol the virtues of the local Tamplins ales, Persil and Guinness. In the distance a double decker bus is approaching on a virtually empty main road which is just as well as the photographer is obviously standing in the road to take this shot. The bus stop seen on the right is reserved for Southdown services only, the other operators in the area being Brighton Hove & District and Brighton Corporation. The viaduct suffered in Brighton's most significant bombing raid of the Second World War when two arches and one pier at the west end of the viaduct, a couple of arches west of the Preston Road span seen here, were demolished and the track left hanging over the void. Prompt temporary repairs had the line operating again 24 hours later – impossible to imagine these days! *RCR4367*

HOVE

50½ miles from London. Frequent Southern Electric express trains from Victoria and London Bridge. Journey time 1 hour.

Although Hove shares with Brighton the long and magnificent seafront, it is nevertheless easy to distinguish where Hove takes over at Brighton's western boundary. Broad lawns, terraces and squares of Regency design replace the long line of hotels and the general impression is one of leafy spaciousness. Hove's great all year round sport and social centre known as the King Alfred includes swimming pools, medicinal baths, restaurant, ballrooms and conference room, an indoor bowls rink, badminton, and facilities for golf and cricket practice. Here, where the majestic Downs come down for a look at the sea and merge with the high cliffs and green hinterland for a few miles, is part of the coast and countryside dear to Kipling and Belloc.

Above: M7 tank No. 30053 makes a spirited getaway from the stop at Hove with a Steyning line service to Horsham in 1958. Although the first station in the area was opened with the line to Shoreham in 1840, this was subsequently closed with the opening of the Cliftonville curve which allowed London trains to avoid reversal at Brighton. A station on the current site was opened in 1865, being named Cliftonville and West Brighton. This was changed to Hove & West Brighton in 1893 before being later changed finally to Hove. The town has always seen itself as distinct from its larger and more boisterous neighbour and despite the joining of the two towns into one unitary authority in 1997 and the subsequent granting of city status in 2001 the answer to the enquiry "Do you live in Brighton?" often elicits the response "No, ... Hove actually". This was elevated into something of a local catchphrase and although it was often used in a humorous vein by most, there was undoubtedly a certain amount of snobbery when used by others. This did not deter Hove Borough Council from subsequently turning it into a slogan in their advertising to attract tourists. The origin of the phrase is believed to derive from a local thespian, one Laurence Olivier. *AEB688*

Opposite top: The headcode carried by T9 No. 30728 in this undated 1956 view indicates that this was the through train from Bournemouth returning to Brighton, having passed non-stop through Hove. That elderly locomotives such as this, (No. 30728 would be withdrawn in October that year,) should continue to be used on through express services to/from Brighton highlights the often chronic availability of the relatively new Bulleid pacifics at 75A resulting in a variety of veteran motive power being substituted. The extensive goods yard can be seen behind the footbridge, access initially being controlled by Hove B signal box situated at the west end of the station. The box seen here, Hove A, was a Saxby & Farmer Type 5 box, similar to Hove B, both being opened in June 1879. It became plain Hove when Hove 'B' closed in 1973. The box, with a frame of 50 levers, continued in use until closure on 17 March 1985. *PH186*

Opposite bottom: One of the elegant Billinton moguls of the K Class, No. 32346, a recent transferee to Brighton shed the previous month, rattles eastwards through Hove with a lengthy goods train on 20 September 1950. The long covered footbridge was primarily a public footpath, there being a subway for railway passengers. There was an extensive goods yard at Hove where in the winter of 1962/3 many steam locomotives from Brighton shed were stored awaiting the final journey to the scrapyard. Following withdrawal of the whole class over just two months at the end of 1962, sadly none of these fine locomotives was preserved. The large building in the centre left background was the Dubarry Perfumery Company which was adorned with mosaic panels in an Art Deco style along the front of the building. In 1962 William R. Warner acquired Dubarry and although the name was maintained in 1964 the company moved from Hove to Hampshire, subsequently going into liquidation in 1982. *RCR4186*

West Sussex

SHOREHAM-BY-SEA

56½ miles from London. Served by Southern Electric express trains from Victoria and London Bridge, in some cases with change of train at Brighton. Journey time approx. 1 hour 20 minutes.

Shoreham-by-Sea's beach, extending for 2 miles and divided from the mainland by the River Adur, is mainly of pebbles, with large tracts of firm sand at low tide. The old town has some interesting churches and other old buildings. Shoreham Harbour is a well known yachting centre and with the River Adur provides good boating and fishing.

In the 1950s relief from the rather monotonous diet of EMUs on the coastal route west of Brighton came in the form of the three through steam hauled services from Brighton to Bournemouth, Plymouth and Cardiff. More regular relief was found in the steam worked Brighton – Horsham service, an example of which is seen here in the shape of M7 No. 30129 halted at the down platform of Shoreham-by-Sea on 31 July 1955. It would appear to have attracted a goodly crowd of passengers wishing to join the train. No. 30129 was based at Brighton shed from July 1953 until June 1956, being transferred to Yeovil where it became a regular performer on the Yeovil Town – Junction shuttle service. In spite of the subsequent introduction of DMUs in June 1964 the branch to Horsham was to close in March 1966. *AEB688*

West Country pacific No. 34027 "Taw Valley" rattles over the level crossing and past Shoreham B signal box with the through train from Plymouth to Brighton on 25 April 1964, whilst a Southdown double decker waits at the crossing. The Plymouth service was one of three steam hauled through services from Brighton in the early 1960s, the others being to Bournemouth and Cardiff but these had ceased running the previous year. The Plymouth service lasted until 1967 when it was cut back to Exeter. No 34027 is still with us being currently housed on the Severn Valley Railway. *FS65-5*

WORTHING

61 miles from London. Served by frequent Southern Electric express trains from Victoria and London Bridge. Journey time approx. 1 hour 20 minutes. Also served by direct through trains from the West of England and South Wales.

Worthing, one of the largest towns in Sussex, is a pleasant residential and all year round holiday resort
and has nearly five miles of sea front with beach fun for all. And what do most parents like better than peaceful relaxation in a deckchair with one somnolent eye on the kiddies? The garden-like appearance of the town is largely due to its many trees and flowery open spaces. Among the principal attractions for children are the Peter Pan Playground, the paddling pool and the boating lake, all in Beach House grounds.

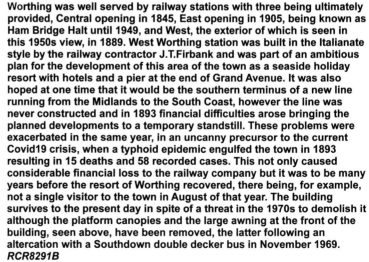

Worthing was well served by railway stations with three being ultimately provided, Central opening in 1845, East opening in 1905, being known as Ham Bridge Halt until 1949, and West, the exterior of which is seen in this 1950s view, in 1889. West Worthing station was built in the Italianate style by the railway contractor J.T.Firbank and was part of an ambitious plan for the development of this area of the town as a seaside holiday resort with hotels and a pier at the end of Grand Avenue. It was also hoped at one time that it would be the southern terminus of a new line running from the Midlands to the South Coast, however the line was never constructed and in 1893 financial difficulties arose bringing the planned developments to a temporary standstill. These problems were exacerbated in the same year, in an uncanny precursor to the current Covid19 crisis, when a typhoid epidemic engulfed the town in 1893 resulting in 15 deaths and 58 recorded cases. This not only caused considerable financial loss to the railway company but it was to be many years before the resort of Worthing recovered, there being, for example, not a single visitor to the town in August of that year. The building survives to the present day in spite of a threat in the 1970s to demolish it although the platform canopies and the large awning at the front of the building, seen above, have been removed, the latter following an altercation with a Southdown double decker bus in November 1969. *RCR8291B*

ANGMERING-ON-SEA

66 miles from London. Served by frequent Southern Electric express trains from Victoria and London Bridge with a change of train at Brighton or Hove. Refreshment car on certain trains.

Angmering-on-Sea is a little garden townlet on the Sussex shore, a place without extremes of heat or cold. It has a profusion of sub tropical plants and flowers giving the whole place a pleasantly Continental atmosphere. Angmering's alter ego, East Preston, is of considerable age and beauty, with picturesque thatched cottages hidden coyly among their green hedges.

One of the famed Brighton Atlantics, No.32425 "Trevose Head", which would be withdrawn the month following this view which was taken on 7 August 1956, showed it was still capable of powering the through train from Brighton to Bournemouth, the location of this shot being Angmering-on-Sea. Another of its final duties was the through service from Hastings to Manchester which it worked as far as Willesden. Badly cracked frames and worn cylinders resulted in the withdrawal of No. 32425 from active service at the end of September but it saw further service as a stationary boiler to provide steam to heat the EMU depot at Slade Green from December 1956 until April 1957 before being scrapped at Brighton Works in August, its birthplace back in 1911. The last Atlantic, "Beachy Head", continued to work on the Brighton-Bournemouth service, even receiving a cylinder plate donated by "Trevose Head" to keep it going until it too was withdrawn at the end of 1957 before its final appearance on an enthusiasts' special in April 1958. In addition to catering for holidaymakers, Angmering was an important market garden and horticultural area where much produce was grown in glasshouses. The Worthing & District Growers' Association co-ordinated the marketing and transport of this and liaised with the railway in the area. Behind the footbridge on the up platform was one of the dedicated covered loading areas for this produce which was conveyed to London in special daily van trains at one time. Similar loading facilities were replicated at other stations in the vicinity. *AEB1534*

HAMPSHIRE

HAYLING ISLAND

71 miles from London. Served by frequent Southern Electric trains from Waterloo to Havant, thence by local train or bus.

Hayling Island is becoming more and more popular, both with those who delight in a quiet and informal

holiday and with those who enjoy the equally informal, yet rather more robust, delights of the holiday camp. The island is linked with the mainland by rail from Havant and by a ferry service connecting it with Portsmouth and Southsea.

Above: Just as one immediately associates Adams Radial tanks with Lyme Regis and Beattie Well tanks at Wadebridge, so the location of Hayling Island invokes memories of the famous Stroudley Class A1X "Terriers", an example of which, No.32662, is seen after arrival at the terminus on 18 August 1963, sadly the final summer of operation. A goodly procession of passengers make their way down the platform to the exit as No. 32662 prepares to run round its train ready for the return to the main line at Havant. Fortunately this example, along with eight others and two designated Class A1, was to survive into preservation, being currently located at the Bressingham Steam Museum. Mention of Lyme Regis brings to mind the fact that No. 32662 worked on this Dorset branch line when on June 28th. 1953 it handled an RCTS special along with Adams tank No. 30583. This was something of a return for the 0-6-0Ts as two "Terriers" had been bought from the LBSCR by the LSWR especially for use on the Lyme Regis branch when it opened in 1903. *RCR17317*

Opposite: No. 32678, with its prominent Westinghouse brake pump mechanism, is seen at the terminus on 14 April 1960 and illustrates its diminutive proportions, weighing in at just 28 tons 5 cwt., when compared to the coaching stock it is about to haul. Along with other class members used on this branch the locomotive sports a wire mesh spark arrestor on its chimney as a precaution against setting fire to the timber trestle bridge which crossed Langstone harbour. In the background can be seen the roof of the Goods Shed, built in 1900 and containing a 30 cwt hand operated crane, which is the only railway building remaining on site today. It has been incorporated into a local theatre used by HIADS - the Hayling Island Amateur Dramatic Society who now tread the boards where once goods were loaded and unloaded. No. 32678 is preserved on the Kent & East Sussex Railway having recently passed her 140th anniversary since construction in 1880. *AEB5257*

Above: The third Terrier featured is No. 32661 seen adjacent to the coaling stage at Hayling on 25 May 1957. The small wooden coal stage constructed from old sleepers located here was supplied from the occasional wagonload of coal brought in by goods or mixed trains. Coal could also be taken on at the small loading stage at Leggett's siding adjacent to the Hayling bay platform at Havant, however water was only available at Havant. Originally named "Sutton", No. 32661 was sought for preservation after withdrawal by BR in April 1963 by the London Borough of Sutton for display at their new Civic Centre to celebrate the part railways played in the development of the town but it was scrapped at Eastleigh Works in September 1963 before the sale could be concluded. In its stead the Borough purchased No. 32650, originally named "Whitechapel", the locomotive being offered on loan to the K&ESR where it operated for many years in the guise of "Sutton". In 2004 Sutton Borough, who still own the locomotive, transferred No. 32650 to the Spa Valley Railway where it is undergoing overhaul. *AEB2129*

PORTSMOUTH & SOUTHSEA

73¾ miles from London. Served by frequent Southern Electric expresses from Waterloo. Journey time approx. 1½ hours with Refreshment Car on many trains. Also served by Southern Electric expresses from Victoria and through expresses from the West of England and South Wales.

Southsea and Portsmouth form another of those delightful twin towns so frequently met with around our shores. What they have in common is their magnificent outlook seawards, where day by day the pageantry of the sea is enacted in its ever changing, yet never changing variety. The sight of the great "Queens" and other liners passing to and from Southampton, and of the lean grey ships of the Royal

Navy at anchor or moving in and out of harbour, with the multi-coloured sails of yachts running before the wind, complete a spectacle of colour and interest of which residents and visitors never tire. In the distance lies the long crest of the Isle of Wight, which protects Southsea from the keen west winds and gives its climate that touch of clemency without robbing it of its tonic and invigorating qualities. At night the promenade is ablaze with coloured fairy lights and illuminated set pieces. Portsmouth can match Southsea in other ways. Its naval associations appeal to that love of the sea which seems inherent in most Englishmen, and the Royal Dockyard and the harbour have an incomparable store of such associations to please the heart and eye.

Opposite bottom: In an echo of summer Saturdays gone by, last day crowds throng the platform at Hayling as No. 32650 runs round its train on the final day of normal services, the 2 November 1963. This was a far cry from the previous year when a 30 minute service operated during summer Saturdays and on a typical Bank Holiday up to 500 passengers/train would disgorge onto Hayling's platform. In the 1930s a new generation of holidaymakers began to discover the delights of Hayling, encouraged no doubt by the fact that a faster service became available from Waterloo and Brighton with electrification although of course the last few miles were always steam powered. The island became one of the first major holiday camp destinations in the UK with a number of local and national camps established from the 1930s onwards and even today there are three sites still operating although of course arrival is now by car or by local bus/taxi for rail travellers from Havant station. No. 32650 had the honour of hauling the final train of the day on the 2nd. November. This train was mixed as the remaining wagons in the goods yard needed to be cleared leaving just enough coal on the coaling stage for the following day's special train double headed by Nos. 32636 and 32670. *RCR17430*

Above: Standard Class 4 2-6-0 No. 76019, carrying a 71A Eastleigh shedplate, awaits departure from platform 5 at Portsmouth and Southsea Low Level on the 6 September 1955. This platform, the longest of those at low level, was often used for the through services to Cardiff and the headcode shown is for the route from Portsmouth to Salisbury via Redbridge. On the far left can be seen the two high level platforms reached via a 1 in 61 gradient which was required to carry the lines to the Harbour station, departure point for the ferries to the Isle of Wight, over Portsmouth's main shopping street, Commercial Road. The station was originally named Portsmouth Town but following the closure of the branch line to Southsea in 1914, at which time passengers and tourists bound for this resort were diverted to Portsmouth Town station, it was subsequently renamed Portsmouth & Southsea in 1925 to reflect its new role. Rationalisation has seen a reduction in the number of platforms at the lower level to just two bays for terminating trains whilst the majority of present day services originate from the Harbour station and therefore utilise the high level platforms. *AEB884*

GOSPORT

77¾ miles from London. Served by frequent Southern Electric express trains from Waterloo to Portsmouth Harbour thence by ferry. Journey time approx. 2 hours.

Gosport, "God's Port", so named in 1140 by Henry of Blois, grandson of William the Conqueror, stands on the western bank of Portsmouth Harbour. Shielded by the Hampshire Downs and the Isle of Wight in winter and laved on two sides by the cool sea in summer, its climate is at once equable and health giving.

Above: On 27 June 1950 a grand old lady in the shape of Class L11 No. 30175, dating from 1903, has cautiously crossed Spring Garden Lane just outside Gosport station, returning from the Royal Navy's establishment at the Royal Clarence Victualling Yard. The train had previously crossed Mumby Road, protected by another set of gates, there being a speed limit of 4 mph across these roads. This example of Drummond's 4-4-0s, from nearby Eastleigh shed, lasted in service until withdrawal at the end of 1951.The BR sign, seen to the right of the fine old VR pillar box, still proudly proclaims this to be Gosport Station as a dwindling passenger service of just a handful of trains per day continued to be provided until June 1953 when they were withdrawn. This was a far cry from the early days when Gosport was the principal station for Portsmouth, hence the rather grand scale of the buildings provided, for some seven years from 1841 until a line to Portsmouth opened from Cosham in 1848. The skeletal appearance of the roof resulted from the replacement of the original timber roof trusses, destroyed in an air raid in March 1941, by steel but the asbestos cladding was applied only to the goods area as seen in this view. This and the rather rundown appearance of the station plus the frequency of local bus services did little to attract passengers, visitors and holidaymakers preferring to catch a train to Portsmouth Harbour and to make the short ferry crossing to Gosport. *RCR4040*

Opposite top: The interior of the station is more clearly revealed in this view taken on 7 March 1959 when an enthusiasts' railtour visited the branch hauled by M7 No. 30111 with push-pull carriage set No. 6. This "Portsmouth Area Railtour" was run by the Branch Line Society and, starting from Portsmouth Harbour, visited Lavant on the former Chichester-Midhurst line, Bishops Waltham, Droxford on the former Meon Valley line and Gosport before returning to Portsmouth Harbour. The carriages comprising the push-pull set were an ex LSWR BCL driving compartment (6496) and an ex SECR compartment second (1103). The platform accommodating the special was the one that had been generally used for passenger traffic in the past whilst the other platform was primarily for goods traffic, the middle line being used for run round purposes. The final special to visit the station was in November 1968 powered by a Class 33, D6506. *AEB4510*

Opposite bottom: The Italianate classical portico and facade of Gosport station is captured on 3 May 1953, a few weeks before passenger closure the following month. The building, by architect Sir William Tite, was constructed by contractor D. Nicholson for the sum of £10,980. It was embellished with fifteen Tuscan columns with Corinthian capitals and coupled chimneys at each end, all of which added up to a very elegant design. It was awarded a Grade II listing and after lying derelict for several decades after closure has now been sympathetically redeveloped to provide residential properties and offices. The notice indicates that "You may park your car at this station" for the sum of 1/- per day and a lone motorist owning an A30, produced by Austin between 1952 – 1956 as an answer to the Morris Minor, seems to have taken advantage of the offer or maybe he is just calling in to enquire about one of the handful of train services on offer by this time. *RCR4505*

LYMINGTON

97½ miles from London. Served by frequent express trains from Waterloo with change of train at Brockenhurst. Journey time 2 ¾ hours.

Lying at the head of a long winding estuary, Lymington occupies a sheltered position on the Solent and enjoys the unusual advantage of double tides. It is consequently a favourite yachting centre. The sight, *from the platform of Lymington Harbour station, of the many yachts moored nearby in the golden haze of a summer morning, with the reflections of the coloured hulls and masts mirrored in the quiet waters, is a picture of colour and security guaranteed to set the brush hand of any artist ecstatically quivering. Lymington Town has an attractive old world air, not surprising considering it was first made a borough as long ago as 1150.*

Above: The attractive exterior of Lymington Town station is shown off to advantage in this view taken on 26 August 1954. The intricate contrasting patterns of brickwork on the gables and over the elegant sash windows were nice architectural touches and although the station today has lost its overall roof the exterior is still very much the same although no longer sporting its "Southern Railway" signage which, even at this date, was some six years after nationalisation. However, the five poster boards were correctly headed "British Railways". This was the terminus of the line from opening in 1858 until the extension to the Pier station was completed in 1884. A somewhat "vertically challenged" lower quadrant signal post, presumably reduced in height to assist sighting under the overall roof, can be seen through the open gate leading to the platform on the far right. RCR5248

Opposite top: The aforementioned overall roof with its unusually tall smoke vents can be seen in some detail in this view taken on 27 August 1954. An M7, No. 30105, the staple motive power on the branch from Brockenhurst to Lymington, is approaching the well filled platform. As the next and final stop was the Pier station most, if not all, of these passengers are probably heading for the Isle of Wight, a sign on the platform warning unwary passengers that it was "Next station for the boats". This veteran 0-4-4T was one of the stud based at Bournemouth depot to cover services on the Lymington line, the Swanage branch and on the "Old Road" via Wimborne. The small engine shed dating from the opening of the line can be seen to the rear of the water column. These Drummond tanks lasted on the Lymington branch until 1964 by which time they were well past their best. No. 30105 was push-pull fitted, like the majority of the class used on the branch, but there was a run round facility available at the Pier station. This example lasted in traffic until withdrawal in May 1963 with the final batch of M7s being withdrawn in May 1964. *RCR5254*

Opposite bottom: And here is one of those "Boats" mentioned on the signboard at the Town station in the shape of the IOW ferry "Lymington" disgorging its relatively small cargo of cars on 26 August 1954. First off is a Standard Vanguard towing a caravan under the watchful gaze of ferry staff directing traffic and some interested spectators. These Vanguards, with their streamlined body shape and six side windows, gave the impression of a contemporary American sedan shrunk to fit British roads for their designer had been instructed to haunt the American Embassy in London and sketch all the American cars that he saw for inspiration. The ferry "Lymington" was built in 1938, being the first British vessel driven by Voith Schneider propulsion units which allowed her to turn in her own length, being somewhat unkindly known locally as "The Crab". By 1972 the ship was considered to be too small and she was bought by Western Ferries where she was renamed "Sound of Sanda" and served as a ferry from Gourock to Dunoon in Scotland from 1974 until 1989 although latterly she was relegated to carrying cement tankers to Faslane whilst the new Trident submarine base was under construction. Attracting no offers for preservation she lay for a number of years in Holy Loch, being eventually sold for use as a support vessel on a fish farm. She was beached to allow conversion work to be carried out but this was never done and she was reduced to a hulk, re-floated and left to rot at a mooring in the loch. A sad end. *RCR5246*

BOURNEMOUTH

108 miles from London. Served by frequent express trains from Waterloo. Journey time 2½ hours. Also served by the "Royal Wessex" and all Pullman "Bournemouth Belle" expresses and direct through express trains from the North, Midlands and South West England.

Bournemouth has been called a sophisticated town. If Bournemouth can be said to approach perfection as far as seaside amenities are concerned and if such a happy state of affairs can be most aptly described by so cumbersome an adjective, there may be some justification for its use. Bournemouth certainly has the

lot, so to speak, but nature supplied most of it, skilfully and felicitously aided and abetted by the local authorities, past and present. It is called the "town of a million pines" and is very easy on the eye not least when the gardens and walks are floodlit and illuminated. Bournemouth's shops match its scenery for elegance and variety and its high class hotels, guest houses and other holiday accommodation are more than adequate. Music and Bournemouth are practically synonymous terms with the world famous Bournemouth Symphony Orchestra, often heard on the air, giving many performances in the Winter Gardens Concert Hall where concerts are also given by other famous orchestras and artistes.

Opposite: M7 No. 30104 has just arrived at journey's end - Lymington Pier station on 10 September 1953. This locomotive was also push-pull fitted so will not need to run round if the carriage stock is one of the push-pull sets usual on this route. The proximity of the station to the Isle of Wight ferries can be gauged by the funnel of one of the ships seen on the far left. The original all timber LSWR signal box seen on the right was superseded by a new brick built box opened in November 1956 positioned about sixty yards north west of the level crossing that was installed in 1938 to allow vehicles to access the ferries. The cattle pens seen behind the signal box were also installed in 1938, for cattle had been transported across the Solent as far back as the 1850s when vessels had run with "tow boats" attached which carried horse drawn carriages and later early motor cars and livestock. *RCR4794*

Above: Waiting to depart under Bournemouth Central's impressive trainshed is the 4.34 pm to Eastleigh hauled by Class H15 No. 30489 on the 9 July 1957. This service called at all stations to Southampton Central and then Eastleigh, leaving a few minutes after departure of the up Bournemouth Belle Pullman service to London. These machines were entering their twilight years by this time with the last examples, including No. 30489 which was built in 1914 as one of the initial batch designed by Robert Urie, being withdrawn in 1961. *LRF2850*

Above: Bournemouth Central's rather smoke grimed overall roof is shown well in this view of King Arthur Class No.30743 "Lyonnesse" taken on 27 June 1954. This 4-6-0 was allocated to Bournemouth depot along with nine other members of the class, from where it would be withdrawn in October the following year although its name would be resurrected when given to Standard Class 5 No. 73113, one of 20 of the class on the SR to receive names, in 1959. The two through roads seen here were removed in late 1966 prior to the Bournemouth electrification scheme of the following year which saw the station renamed plain Bournemouth, the former Bournemouth West station having been closed in 1966. The station building was listed Grade II in 1974 and following damage in the great storm of 1987 the roof was refurbished in 2000 and now looks far better than it did in steam days. *RCR5166*

Bottom: The aforementioned "Bournemouth Belle", resplendent with headboard, departs Bournemouth Central on 30 May 1953 with very unusual motive power at the head in the shape of ex LNER Gresley V2 2-6-2 No.60893. The use of such exotic traction was down to the accident which had recently occurred at Crewkerne with Merchant Navy 35020 "Bibby Line" when it fractured an axle resulting in the whole class being withdrawn for ultrasonic checks. A further shot of a V2 hauled Bournemouth Belle, this time at Waterloo, appears in a companion volume in this series - "Southern Medley". *RCR4625*

Above: Bournemouth shed, 71B, and after recoding in September 1963 70F, was adjacent to Central station and hosted steam and diesel traction until the end of steam on the SR on 9 July 1967. This view taken on 4 June 1967 shows rebuilt Bulleid pacific No. 34034, which formerly carried the name "Honiton", in company with an unidentified Standard and a Class 33 diesel. No. 34034 lasted in service until the 1st. July, being withdrawn from Nine Elms shed just a few days before steam's finale. It was subsequently stored at its home shed until transferred to Salisbury for a further period being one of the final trio of locomotives to leave the Salisbury dumping ground for Cashmore's scrapyard in Newport, South Wales, on 30 March the following year. Class 33s continued to power services from Bournemouth to Weymouth until completion of electrification to Weymouth in 1988. *A Swain V92-2*

Bottom: Bournemouth's other main station was designated Bournemouth West which served as the terminus for through holiday trains via the Somerset & Dorset line as well as those from Waterloo. It was also the starting point for local trains to Brockenhurst and Salisbury via Broadstone. One of Bournemouth depot's Drummond M7 tanks, No. 30059 which lasted in service until February 1961, is acting as station pilot in this undated view. *NS200801A*

Dorset

POOLE

113¾ miles from London. Served by express trains from Waterloo. Journey time approx. 3 hours. Also served by direct through expresses from the West, South Wales, Midlands and North.

Poole is the largest town in Dorset. Its climate combines the warmth of the south with the exhilaration of the west. There are fine parks and promenades, excellent shops, restaurants and cafes, *fragrant pinewoods and facilities for every form of sport and recreation. Poole is a grand spot for the children, with over 3,000 acres of parks and open spaces. Poole Park, for example, has a salt water lake covering 60 acres and only 3½ feet deep, also facilities for all kinds of games. Poole has memories and mementoes of the past and the older parts of the town are well worth a visit. So are the pottery and china establishments.*

Opposite: Standard tank No. 82026 enters the curving platforms of Poole station from the west with the 12.09pm service from Brockenhurst to Bournemouth West via Wimborne on 11 April 1964. Bournemouth shed had four consecutively numbered examples of these 3MT 2-6-2Ts on their books at this time although they would all be transferred away in August of that year following closure of the lines from Bournemouth to both Brockenhurst and Salisbury via Broadstone on 4 May. *FS50-3*

Above: Approaching the station from the other direction, Class U mogul No. 31792 negotiates the two level crossings which were situated in close proximity at the eastern end of the station with the 1.03pm service from Bournemouth West to Salisbury also on the 11 April 1964. Whilst the further crossing is still in situ today the nearer one was replaced by a bridge in 1971 and Poole's Victorian station buildings replaced by prefabricated structures in the 1970s which were themselves replaced by more permanent structures in the late 1980s. In steam days Poole was the largest town, by population in Dorset. That accolade has now moved to Bournemouth in consequence of county boundary changes. *FS50-5*

SWANAGE

132 miles from London. Served by express trains, including the "Royal Wessex" from Waterloo with change of train at Wareham. (In certain cases there are through carriages.) Journey time 3¾ hours.

Swanage, lying snugly in a magnificent bay, has a climate both bracing and mild, with a high sunshine record and low rainfall. Swanage is indeed favoured by nature and beloved by residents and visitors alike. It is the "Knollsea" of Thomas Hardy's Wessex. The town is expanding rapidly, particularly in the New Swanage area. Swanage has a long history. Here Alfred the Great defeated the Danes in the first recorded English naval victory in 877. The carved facade of the Town hall, designed by Sir Christopher Wren, once graced the front of Mercers' Hall in Cheapside.

One of the footplate crew waves from the cab of M7 No. 30056 as, with safety valves lifting, it makes a spirited getaway from the terminus at Swanage in April 1953 passing the LSWR signal box with a service for the main line at Wareham. M7s were the mainstay of services on the branch for over 30 years with the final examples of these Drummond 0-4-4Ts not being withdrawn from service on the region until May 1964. This scene has of course been recreated in preservation with M7 No. 30053 having been repatriated from the USA to operate over the Swanage Railway since 1992. FH818

WEYMOUTH

142¾ miles from London. Served by express trains from Waterloo and Paddington. Journey time 3¾ hours from Waterloo and 4 hours from Paddington. Refreshment Car on several trains.

Weymouth was not always a flourishing holiday resort, it was an ancient port and borough and preserves much of its old world atmosphere, not only in some of its narrow streets and quaint old houses, but also in the harbour which, for all its modern activity, is still reminiscent of less hectic days when Weymouth was known primarily as a fishing and seaport town. Nowadays, fine steamers arriving from or sailing to the Channel Islands are the predominant users of the harbour, but the brown sailed fishing smacks, yachts and other small craft help to preserve some of the old time characteristics. The roomy beach can accommodate thousands of people and other attractions include beauty competitions, talent contests, roller skating revues and greyhound racing.

Top: Merchant Navy pacific No. 35024 "East Asiatic Company" has charge of the 5.15 pm service to Bournemouth Central on 14 August 1960. The shedcode on the smokebox door reads 71B indicating that it was allocated to Bournemouth shed which had eight of these 8P locomotives on their books at this time. This example had been rebuilt the year before this view was taken and was to last in service until January 1965. A rake of Bulleid coaches can be seen at the adjacent platform sporting carriage boards reading "Waterloo – Southampton - Weymouth". The locomotive's namesake shipping company was founded in 1897 in Copenhagen and initially operated services between Copenhagen, Bangkok and the Far East. In the early 1920s they extended services from Copenhagen to South Africa, Cuba, Australia, Mexico and a variety of North Pacific ports but with the advent of air travel passenger sailings gradually diminished until they were discontinued in 1969. *WS4193*

Bottom: Whilst Weymouth attracted many holidaymakers in its own right it was also the departure point for the Channel Islands steamers, one of which is seen here berthed alongside Weymouth Quay station on 24 July 1958. The vessel is the TSS (Twin screw steamship) "St. Helier" registered in Weymouth and built for the GWR in 1925 for the crossing to the Channel Islands. In 1939 she was transferred to Fishguard but was requisitioned by the military and took part in the Dunkirk evacuation. She then transported prisoners of war from Gourock to the Isle of Man detention centres. After a spell at Dartmouth, where she was converted to an assault ship, she took part in the D day landings. After the war she returned to Weymouth and served here until the end of 1960 before being withdrawn and broken up at Antwerp. Ferries to the Channel Islands from Weymouth ceased in March 2015 when the latest operators, Condor, moved their departure point to Poole. The pannier tank, one of only two GWR classes of this type with outside cylinders, seen alongside is No. 1370, one of the 1365 Class of Collett 0-6-0PTs designed especially for docksides and other lines where curvatures were often tight. It was the first of the half dozen members of its class to be withdrawn in January 1960, not being fortunate enough to be one of the trio that were transferred to Wadebridge to replace the Beattie well tanks in 1962. A fine array of vintage vehicles, fortunately parked to give the locomotive sufficient clearance which was often a problem on this quayside tramway, completes the attractive scene. In February 2020 it was reported that £1.1 million had been allocated by the Department for Transport to facilitate the removal of the quayside tramway track, estimated to cost £1.5m in total, which was considered to be in such a bad state that it was no longer usable. *RCR1248A*

Below: Weymouth's motive power depot was situated at a little distance from the station and was opened in 1885. Coded 82F under the WR in 1950 it was re-coded 71G in February 1958 upon transfer to the SR, the final recoding being 70G effective from March 1963 until closure in July 1967. Bulleid West Country pacific No. 34002 "Salisbury" is seen by the coaling stage prior to returning the LCGB "Green Arrow" special from Weymouth to Waterloo on 3 July 1966, double heading with Black 5 No. 45493 as far as Bournemouth. It had previously worked the special from London to Salisbury in place of the failed "Green Arrow" Class V2 No. 60919 which had been brought down from Dundee especially for the trip. Weymouth depot was to be one of the collection points for redundant steam locomotives after July 1967 although No. 34002 did not make it to the end being withdrawn in April of that year. *A Swain U87-2*

LYME REGIS

151½ miles from London. Served by express trains from Waterloo to Axminster with change of train or bus connection. Journey time approx. 4 hours.

Lyme Regis, a pleasant little all season resort on the Dorset Devon border, sheltered from the north and north east winds, has glorious golden sands, perfectly safe for bathing at all times, with hundreds of pools left at low tide to delight the young yachtsmen and shrimpers. The harbour, shielded by the famous Cobb, is filled in summer with yachts and boats of all kinds and many trips can be made from it to neighbouring ports. The interesting Museum contains much to delight the geologist and there is good entertainment on offer at the Marine Theatre, Regent Cinema and Woodmead Dance Hall.

Opposite top: Think of the Lyme Regis branch and one immediately thinks of the Adams radial tanks, a trio of which kept services running for many years ever since their first appearance on the branch in 1913. Other types had worked the line in the past such as A1Xs, O2s and D1s but it was the radials which one always associated with the branch. No. 30582, built by Stephenson's and dating from 1885, is seen on 23 July 1958 making an energetic departure from the terminus with a 2 coach train for the main line junction at Axminster. Like Sidmouth, the station here was rather inconvenient for the town and seafront, being some 250 feet above sea level and more than ½ mile up a long hill from the main street although LSWR publicity naturally concentrated on the downhill journey from the station stating that "Less than 10 minutes' walk is sufficient to bring the visitor right on to the sea front." The sylvan setting of the station is apparent in this view and being at such an elevation above the town passengers could obtain a tantalising glimpse of the sea away to the left as they arrived. *RCR12461*

Bottom: The 14 July 1960 turned out to be a gorgeous summer's day, obviously shirtsleeve weather judging by the shunter's attire, and the photographer, Dick Riley in this case, made the most of his visit to Lyme Regis where he captured the second radial of the trio, No. 30583, engaged in some light shunting. Adjacent to the small goods shed, which was moved from its original position in the 1920s and now appears to be supported on baulks of timber, 30583's crew happily pose for the picture. Lined black livery seemed to suit these elegant locomotives and No. 30583 carries the second style of BR crest introduced in 1957. The usual freight traffic associated with a branch line such as coal, building materials, fertiliser and general merchandise arrived in vans such as the one being toyed with by the locomotive, the vans being dropped off outside the station and letting gravity do the rest. For a number of years the local branch of Boots the chemist received their own dedicated van from their Nottinghamshire headquarters. Saved for preservation on the Bluebell Railway, No. 30583 had remarkably achieved a mileage in excess of 2 million by the time of its withdrawal. *RCR15020*

Opposite top: The final example of the Adams tanks to be seen on the branch was No. 30584, captured here at Lyme on 11 April 1959. Having been constructed by Dubs & Co in 1885 this veteran was in its 75th year by the date of this photograph. With no turning facilities available return workings to Axminster were undertaken, as here, bunker first. The coach carries a destination board "Lyme Regis Branch", no doubt useful information for the general public but with an Adams radial on the train, enthusiasts understood that this could really be nowhere else on the BR system. *AEB4615*

Opposite bottom: On July of the same year No. 30584 is still hard at work having brought a service from Axminster to a halt at Lyme's platform on the 8th of that month. The locomotive will pull forward and, using the run round facility, proceed to the head of the train for the return working, taking water if required from the crane positioned outside the small locomotive shed which remained open until the introduction of DMUs to the line in November 1963. Following withdrawal in January 1961 No. 30584 was scrapped at Eastleigh Works in December of that year. *RCR13789*

Above: 1961 witnessed the replacement of the ageing Adams tanks with more modern locomotion in the form of Ivatt tanks. No. 41318 of that ilk is seen on 4 July 1961 awaiting time for its bunker first departure for Axminster under the fascinated gaze of a little boy whilst a couple say their fond platform edge farewells. The stock consists of just a single coach to a 1930s Maunsell design. These were useful 'loose' coaches which could be coupled to a Corridor Open Second to form two coach sets, Nos.104-107/9/10. These often saw service on West Country branches such as Exmouth, Sidmouth, Callington and here at Lyme Regis. Somewhat against usual SR policy it was agreed on the Lyme Regis branch that sets could be split according to demand and that a train could operate with just a brake composite as is apparent here. Even in July, one of the peak holiday months, as pictured here, the branch could only muster sufficient patronage for what was surely a grossly uneconomic working with a driver, fireman and guard all required to look after a handful of passengers. These powerful tank locomotives could haul five coaches unassisted when required over this undulating heavily graded route, realising some savings in operating costs through dispensing with double heading and enabling through coaches from Waterloo to continue to visit the line until 1963. The Ivatts enjoyed a virtual monopoly of services for the next couple of years although Standard Class 2 tanks also made appearances on the branch from time to time. *RCR13984*

Above: A few passengers await the arrival of Lyme's final motive power in the form of DMUs, in this case three single cars, approaching the terminus in the final year of operation with a service from Axminster. Steam did occasionally deputise for failed DMUs as late as March 1965 during a shortage of diesel units although this was eased by the transfer of the single car formerly used on the Halwill-Torrington service, No. W55000, following closure of that line from 1 March. Just a run round loop remained at this time for emergency use and sleepers clearly indicate where former track had been recovered, the goods yard having closed in February 1964. Following Exmouth Junction shed's loss of its final steam allocation in May 1965 any further steam working on the Lyme branch was rendered unlikely so the remaining run round facilities, signalling and ground frame at Lyme were all taken out of use. The branch, very much reduced to a "basic railway", closed with final services running on 27 November 1965. *C305*

Opposite top: Combpyne sees some custom as passengers make their way out of the station as No. 30582 prepares to get under way to Axminster and the main line on 20 July 1958. As can be appreciated from this view the platform was situated on a tight curve and it was such curves as these, in which the line abounded, that ensured the longevity of these Adams radial tanks. They lasted in service until the newer and more powerful Ivatt tanks were tested on the branch following the easing of some of the curves and substantial track renewal in 1960. The locomotive in the worst condition, No. 30584, was withdrawn in January 1961 followed by the remaining pair prior to that year's summer season but, as is well known, No. 30583 was thankfully preserved on the Bluebell Railway. *RCR12394*

Opposite bottom: At Combpyne the branch swung away from an east-west alignment followed from Uplyme to head northwards towards Axminster. No. 30584 is at the head of this up service captured on 11th. April 1959. As the station had no mains water supply this had to be delivered by rail in churns, one of which can just be seen to the left of the platform trolley in front of the porter. There appears to be a car parked next to the Camping Coach seen on the left parked on a siding which once formed part of a loop line. These Camping Coaches were first introduced by the LNER in the summer of 1933 and the idea was taken up by the SR in 1935 when twelve were installed at various locations, the season running from April to September. Combpyne did not receive its first coach until 1947, this being an ex LC&DR 6 wheeler. This was replaced in 1954 by the vehicle seen here, an ex LSWR 56 foot bogie non corridor composite constructed at Eastleigh in 1906. This vehicle lasted in service here until the end of the season in 1963. Charges in the late 1950s were £5 15s /week (low season) rising to £9 in the peak season. Access to the interior was pretty rudimentary, being by means of the ladder seen propped against the coach door. The coach would return to Eastleigh at the end of each season for maintenance. *AEB4616*

Devon

COMBPYNE

149 miles from London. Served by express trains from Waterloo with change of train at Axminster. Journey time approx. 3¾ hours.

On the Axminster – Lyme Regis branch line, Combpyne is a pleasant village, only a mile from the seashore, which is bounded by wooded cliffs.

Combpyne is the nearest station for the Landslip, a wild area covered by trees and bushes, traversed by a rough four mile long pathway. A Camping Coach is stationed here and can be rented for one or two weeks. In addition to the rental, tenants must purchase in advance ordinary return rail tickets from their home station. The demand for these coaches is extremely heavy and early booking is recommended.

CAMPING COACHES

COMBPYNE

Opposite top: The sight of double heading on the branch was a sure sign that one of the through services from Waterloo was being hauled over the switchback route to its final destination at Lyme. Here Nos. 30583 (leading) and 30582 (train engine) have charge of just such a service on 26 July 1958. The load for one of these 4-4-2Ts unassisted was three coaches but six could be accommodated when two locomotives were provided. Normally the through coaches were added to the branch set or in one case, the 10:45 am from Waterloo to Seaton, five through coaches were worked from Axminster as a complete train. Combpyne's running in board had formerly advertised "For the Landslip", referring to the nearby Dowlands Cliffs landslip which occurred in December 1839 and was to become a tourist attraction in its own right with the central plateau of the slip being known as Goat Island and the ravine formed, which is now heavily overgrown, given the name The Chasm. Remarkably a crop of wheat sown on the section of land that had slipped was successfully harvested the following summer. Apart from the Landslip there was little in the vicinity to generate much traffic, the small village of Combpyne (Pop. 101 in 1901 and only 321 in the mid 1950s) was nearly ¾ mile down a hill from the station. In addition to the resident Camping Coach a solitary van occupies the siding which was formerly a passing loop but was converted to a dead end in August 1921. The occasional van would often contain fertiliser in bags for local agricultural use. A solitary bench provides the only passenger facility on the platform itself, the overly large station buildings being located off the picture to the left. A Stationmaster was in residence here until 1930 after which a porter sufficed. *RCR12487*

Opposite bottom: With Combpyne station building and separate platform visible in the distance, No. 30584 enters the cutting to the east of the station on 9 July 1959 with a single coach service to Lyme. This view was taken from an overbridge which carried the road from Rousdon to Axminster. For such an insignificant location Combpyne enjoyed quite a reasonable train service with nine journeys each way on Mondays-Fridays in the summer of 1962 for example, with an extra service on Saturdays being the through coaches from/to Waterloo. The gradient was 1 in 200 up on entering the station but changed to 1 in 40 down towards Cannington Viaduct. *RCR13794*

Above: Although not featuring a resort station, I could not resist inclusion of this atmospheric view of an Adams 0415 tank crossing the graceful 10 arch Cannington Viaduct located a mile or so before its booked stop at Combpyne. The train is the 3:55 pm from Lyme Regis to Axminster and has No. 30584 at its head, the date being 27 August 1954. Thirteen minutes were allowed for the 2½ mile uphill slog from Lyme to Combpyne which included a couple of stretches of 1 in 40 and observance of a 25 mph speed restriction over the viaduct. The building on the left of this view is Shapwick Grange Farm which stands alone in the isolated Cannington Valley formed by one of the headwaters of the River Lim, the crossing of which by the railway necessitated the construction of the viaduct. When it opened in 1903 this was one of the earliest examples of this type of major construction in concrete in the south of England and in spite of structural fears, leading to the construction of a supporting jack arch, the viaduct still stands firm today being Grade II listed. The Bridport News of 28th .August 1903 described the country that may be seen from the train around Shapwick Grange farm as "a pretty spot where may be seen lowing herds of red Devon cattle browsing almost knee deep in the luxuriant meadows of the Cannington valley." No cattle apparent in this view but there is a line of washing hanging out to dry behind the farm but this is probably far enough away from the track to avoid "smuts" emitted by the locomotives, the bane of many a lineside housewife. *RCR5263*

SEATON

152¼ miles from London. Served by express trains from Waterloo with change of train at Seaton Junction (in certain cases through carriages). Journey time approx. 4 hours.

Seaton is the easternmost resort in Devon. It combines a tonic element with the mild South Devon climate. Although there are many enjoyable cliff walks and rides, there are wide stretches of promenades and walks on level ground, which enable even the older people, semi-invalids and those convalescing from illness to get their share of health giving exercise without trouble and anxiety. From the sheltered hollow through which the River Axe flows to meet the sea, Seaton looks out to a wide bay, girdled by a magnificent line of cliffs. To the east of the bay is the Landslip, a pleasant rendezvous for picnic parties. Seaton has excellent facilities for sports and games and the visits of many famous cricket touring teams during the late summer afford much pleasure to visitors and residents.

Opposite: M7 No. 30046 is seen at Seaton terminus on 5 May 1957 with a return service to Seaton Junction where connection was made with the main line. These Drummond tanks had for many years provided the usual motive power on the line and indeed the Seaton branch was to be the last in East Devon to be regularly worked by these 0-4-4Ts, 1962 being their final full year of traditional operation. The last recorded working by an M7 occurred on 2 May 1963 when No. 30048 was in action. The small locomotive shed, coaling stage and water tower seen here comprised the servicing facilities available at Seaton. The engine shed was constructed of Muribloc concrete blocks in 1936, replacing an earlier wooden structure, and concrete components, manufactured by the Southern's Exmouth Junction Concrete Works, were used in the new coaling stage and as supports for the water tower, these supports being in fact standard footbridge components. Some cattle pens can just be seen between the coaling stage and the loco shed which was closed on 4 November 1963. Shed staff based here comprised a shedman, two drivers and two firemen. Excursion traffic had at one time been heavy with an estimated 5,000 passengers arriving by rail on Whit Monday in 1900 for example. The construction of a Warners holiday camp near to the station in the 1930s and of a later rival camp next to it, which was later amalgamated into Warners, naturally boosted rail traffic but, by the time the end of services came in March 1966, a single unit diesel railcar was more than adequate for the remaining traffic. The holiday camp was subsequently demolished and a supermarket now occupies the site. *AEB2092*

Above: An interesting collection of coaching stock was to be seen at Seaton on 17 July 1957. Two car set No. 381, a former LSWR Ironclad set built under Maunsell in 1925, waits at the main platform ready for its next sojourn up the 4½ mile branch to Seaton Junction. Although originally intended to work on the London to Lymington route, in 1949 set 381, which consisted of Third Brake No. 4052 and Composite Brake No.6560, was converted for push-pull working and transferred to the Seaton branch. Alterations were made to the vehicles, such that some luggage space in the Third Brake was sacrificed to provide an additional compartment and the lavatory was reconfigured to provide a six seat coupé whilst the Composite Brake merely had the lavatory changed to a similar six seat coupé. Standard driving ends were fitted to the brake end of each coach with a droplight in each ducket and the gangway connections were removed. On the right are some more modern vehicles in the shape of BR mark 1 stock probably waiting to form a through service to Waterloo, Seaton continuing to be served by through services from the capital until 1963. In this year three services were provided leaving Waterloo on summer Saturdays at 8:03 am, 9:00 am and 10:45 am with two return workings leaving Seaton at 10:20 am and 2:35 pm. Certainly the most interesting vehicle is the single coach parked on the left on an isolated length of track. Remarkably this was a twelve wheeled 65 ft. 6 in. 41 ton former LNWR clerestory sleeping car built in 1904 as one of fifteen constructed for West Coast Joint stock. It had been converted to provide staff messing/sleeping facilities in 1949, painted light grey and numbered in the Departmental series DM198931. Similar vehicles were to be found at Wadebridge, Launceston, Bude and at Lyme Regis where DM 198930 was used by crews overnight on relief turns from Exmouth Junction shed. Following scrapping of the vehicle at Lyme in 1958 staff resorted to sleeping in the goods shed where there were bunks to accommodate three, the porter apparently dishing out bed linen. *LRF230*

SIDMOUTH

167¾ miles from London. Served by express trains, including the "Atlantic Coast Express" from Waterloo with a change of train at Sidmouth Junction (in certain cases through carriages). Journey time approx. 4 hours.

Sidmouth nestles between two grand headlands, Peak Hill and Salcombe Hill, with lower hills stretching away on either side. To this protection Sidmouth owes much of its reputation for warmth. Indeed Sidmouth was one of the earliest of our resorts to claim recognition as an all season resort. The Duke of Connaught, brother of King Edward VII, paid many visits to Sidmouth for health reasons and the gardens on the western cliff bear his name. They afford sheltered, flowery walks and a good view commanding the bay. Sidmouth was once a port of some importance and there is still good sea fishing to be had with locally caught lobsters and crabs obtainable in shops and on the streets.

Above: Drummond M7 0-4-4Ts had for many years held sway on the former LSWR branch lines in East Devon and this example, No. 30044, was captured standing by Sidmouth's signal box on 24 July 1958. At the start of this year there were still 99 examples in service, the final batch not being withdrawn until 1964. No. 30044 was a long time Exmouth Junction shed resident and was not one of those fitted for push pull working, thereby necessitating running round at the end of each trip. An interesting feature apparent in this view is the private siding visible in the background, which ran behind the signal box, and led to the site of the former gasworks which had closed in 1956. Between 1958 and closure of the branch, vehicles for the firm of J. P. White, who manufactured motor caravan conversions called Devon Caravettes based on Volkswagen vans, were delivered by rail from the importers based in Ramsgate. Sadly the founder, Jack White, died of a heart attack at the wheel of a VW pickup at the factory in 1963 at the age of 51. The company was sold but continued to trade under the J. P. White name until 1971 when it was renamed Devon Conversions Ltd. By the following year the company had become the official VW convertor for the whole UK with sales of over 3,500 vehicles per year and models named the Torvette, Eurovette, Sunlander, Devonette, Continental, Sundowner and Moonraker were being produced. 1981 saw the company relocate to Exeter but in 1985 it unfortunately went into voluntary liquidation. *RCR12432*

Opposite top: Standard Class 3 2-6-2T No. 82019 pulls away bunker first from Sidmouth's platform 2 with set No. 24 and a strengthening Bulleid coach bound for Sidmouth Junction on 13 October 1959. Designed at Swindon, forty-five of this class were introduced from 1952. This example, along with nine other members of the class, was allocated to Exmouth Junction shed at this date for local suburban and branch line work. Platform 2 was the shorter of the two platforms available at Sidmouth, being able to accommodate just five coaches whereas the longer platform 1 could hold seven vehicles. Of interest are the unusually long finials on the LSWR wooden bracket signal post fitted with SR upper quadrant arms and the contrasting types of ground signal, that on the right also being of SR design. These Standard Class 3s, along with Standard Class 4 and Ivatt tank locomotives, replaced the M7s which had formerly had a monopoly on the Sidmouth branch but the reign of these newer designs was to be short lived with DMUs taking over at the end of 1963. *RCR14369*

Bottom: Unlike those at neighbouring Seaton and Exmouth, which remained in use until the end of steam working, Sidmouth's former locomotive shed built in 1900, following destruction of the former wooden structure by fire, fell out of use in the 1930s and access was blocked off as seen here on 13 July 1960. Noteworthy is the Mark 1 coach, E15722, a long way from its native Eastern Region which had undoubtedly arrived on that famous, or should that be infamous, long distance through train from Cleethorpes to Exmouth introduced in the year of this view running via Bath Green Park and Templecombe. It only operated on Saturdays for three summer seasons and as the journey from the Lincolnshire coast to the Devon coast at Sidmouth took seventeen minutes over ten hours it must have been somewhat of an endurance test. It was this type of uneconomic holiday working which was anathema to Dr. Beeching with stock being utilised on just one day a week lying idle until the return working the following Saturday. After closure the shed found a new use being taken over for a time by the Sidmouth Engineering Co. Ltd., a manufacturer of iron gates. To entice the holidaymaker Sidmouth had the added attraction of a railway owned hotel just down the road from the station in the form of The Knowle, a 60 bedroom establishment. Built in 1809 as a country house it became a hotel in 1882. Following requisition by the RAF during WW2, becoming known as RAF Sidmouth, it was bought by the Southern Railway in 1947. Somewhat surprisingly the BTC Hotels Group decided to sell the hotel, along with the GWR Manor House hotel in Moretonhampstead, in the summer of 1951. The hotel finally closed in 1968 and was sold to the local council, becoming their offices. It is currently due to be redeveloped as assisted living for the elderly. *RCR14998*

The Goods Shed, with its attached Goods Office seen here, contained a two ton crane, the jib of which can just be glimpsed in this July 1960 view. Coal, as evidenced by the heaps of loose coal and the sacks neatly stacked on the right of the picture, was a major traffic here but building materials, general merchandise and agricultural items were also important. A British Railways van in crimson and cream livery is being filled with fuel utilising a supply in the yard, requiring it to be pumped by hand by a BR employee. Two other lorries are visible in the yard and at the far end to the right of the guard's van a Ford 8 car can just be identified, no doubt belonging to the signalman who wished to keep an eye on it from his nearby box. The Goods Yard, which was not capable of site expansion, was rather cramped containing just three sidings which were also used to stable coaching stock on occasions. *RCR14990*

The exterior of the attractive station building at Sidmouth on 13 July 1960 reveals a Morris Minor convertible (the photographer, Dick Riley's perhaps?), a Royal Mail Morris J type 10cwt van and a motor cycle parked on the forecourt. These Royal Mail vehicles were produced between 1949 and 1961 and the Post Office purchased 6,000 examples for postal and engineering duties. Sadly mail is no longer carried by rail. The primary disadvantage of the station in this seaside resort was the distance from the shore – 200 feet above sea level and almost a mile from the town centre and esplanade, necessitating buses or taxis to transfer passengers and their luggage to/from their hotels. This compared unfavourably with the situation of nearby Seaton station which was virtually on the sea front. The choice of location for Sidmouth station was no doubt a combination of geography plus Victorian sensibilities about allowing hordes of trippers into their rather select resort. For the holidaymaker who could face the uphill jaunt to the station from their hotel there was the chance to explore the local area by train, purchasing one of the three available Holiday Runabout tickets that included Sidmouth. Area 12 gave access to Lyme Regis, Chard, Seaton, Budleigh Salterton, Exmouth and Exeter Central whilst Area 14, with Sidmouth as its westernmost point, allowed travel to Seaton, Lyme Regis, Chard and Thornfalcon on the Chard Junction-Taunton branch, Yeovil, Martock on the Yeovil-Taunton branch and Sherborne. Area 20 gave access to Honiton, Exmouth, Torquay, Brixham, Kingswear and Totnes with an additional option of adding river trips on the River Dart between Totnes and Dartmouth/Kingswear. During the period 27 April to 25 October 1958 for example one of these tickets could be had for the princely sum of 20/- (£1), being valid for seven days travel from Sunday to the following Saturday which was convenient as most holiday bookings ran from Saturday to Saturday. However, there was the caveat that *"No allowance or extension of date can be granted on these tickets in consequence of there being no Sunday service in certain cases."* RCR14999

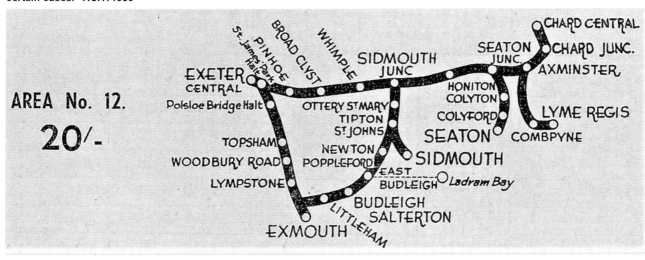

BUDLEIGH SALTERTON

171 miles from London. Served by express trains from Waterloo with change of train at Sidmouth Junction (in certain cases through carriages). Journey time approx. 4 hours.

Budleigh Salterton, between Sidmouth and Exmouth, is one of those resorts which seems to have been *slipped in "betwixt and between". Yet it is a charming little town, unspoilt but quite up to date. The pebble beach extends in a shallow bay for three glorious miles from Otterhead in the east to beyond the Beacon in the west. Here the typically red cliffs rise to a height of nearly 500 feet. Among the special summer events are bowls and tennis tournaments, both of which attract some of the best known players.*

A very clean Standard 2-6-2T, No. 82025, runs round its short working from Exmouth, consisting of two coaches and a van, which was due to terminate at Budleigh Salterton at 6:29 pm on the 9 July 1959. The platforms can be seen through the graceful three arch overbridge at the east end of the station. Nine minutes were allowed before the booked return departure at 6:38 pm which called at Littleham and Exmouth, which was reached in just twelve minutes. Budleigh, like many East Devon resorts, had a shingle beach which did not always find favour with sand loving family holidaymakers and day trippers but the town had its own quiet charms and was well served by the railway in the year of this view with thirteen departures daily to Exmouth and ten to Tipton St. Johns, where connections could be made for Sidmouth and/or Sidmouth Junction. The line from Tipton St. John's, which had originally terminated at Budleigh, was extended to Exmouth by the LSWR in 1903 enabling much of the through traffic from London to Exmouth to be diverted this way thus reducing congestion at Exeter. Freight services ceased in January 1964 with passenger closure coming on 6 March 1967. *RCR13797*

LITTLEHAM

174 miles from London. Served by express trains including the "Atlantic Coast Express" with change of train at Sidmouth Junction (in certain cases through carriages). Journey time approx. 4 hours.

Littleham is a village 1¾ miles from Exmouth. The church is of considerable interest, since it is claimed to be the oldest in this part of Devon. The chancel, dating from 1234, is part of the original building. In the churchyard is the grave of Lady Nelson, wife of the great admiral.

On the 24 May 1961 photographer Leslie Freeman travelled on the 4:44 pm service from Tipton St. Johns to Exmouth hauled by Standard tank No. 82013. Leaning from a carriage window he took a shot of the train as it departed from Littleham and traversed the level crossing at the west end of the station. Three adults and a child seem to comprise the sum total of the alighting passengers. The small platform sited signal box seen here had recently received a matching extension to enable the station to be staffed by one man with, as the hanging sign indicates, a ticket office being provided. At this time Littleham was very much separate from Exmouth, into whose sprawl it has subsequently been subsumed, and was obviously felt to be a sufficiently attractive location to warrant the placing of Camping Coaches in the yard to the rear of the signal box for a number of seasons. *LRF5690*

EXMOUTH

175¾ miles from London. Served by express trains including the "Atlantic Coast Express" from Waterloo. In certain cases through carriages or change of train at either Exeter Central or Sidmouth Junction. Journey time approx. 4 hours. Also served by direct through trains from the North, Midlands and South Wales with changes of train at Exeter St. David's and Exeter Central.

The splendid golden sands which provide safe bathing, and which have helped to make Exmouth so popular for family holidays, extend for 3 miles to Orcombe Point and beyond to Sandy Bay and Straight Point. Set in lovely sunken gardens is the Pavilion where plays and concerts are given and dances are held. Much of Exmouth is built on rising ground and those energetic enough can sample the fine air and splendid views from the grassy topped red cliffs to eastward. There is plenty to watch from a seat in the gardens or along the esplanade. Exmouth is famous for its sunsets set against the blue shadowed Haldon Hills across the estuary. Many famous artists have been lured to this spot by these and other unusual manifestations of natural beauty.*

Above: Having previously arrived from Exeter, Drummond M7 0-4-4T No. 30323 and 3 coach suburban set No. 154 plus a "loose" vehicle await a return working to Exeter from Exmouth's platform No. 1 on 12 October 1959. This spacious four platform terminus dated from 1924, superseding the original station opened in 1862, with platforms 1 and 2 generally reserved for Exeter services whilst 3 and 4 served the line to Tipton St. Johns. This M7, a long time Exmouth Junction shed resident, was withdrawn just a couple of months after this view was taken at the end of 1959 after a working life of almost 60 years. Carriage sets Nos. 152-155, which regularly worked on the Exmouth branch, were BR Mk1 non-gangwayed stock dating from 1954 and had long, 63 ft. 5 in. underframes similar to other BR Mk1 standard stock. They consisted of a Brake Second, Composite and a further Brake Second and appeared on the SR in crimson livery and later in green and were often allied to a single "loose" coach to make up a 4 coach train when demand warranted. *RCR14352*

Opposite top: More modern motive power in the form of Ivatt tank No. 41306 is at the head of an Exeter service a day later on 13 October 1959. Along with platform No. 4 this platform, No. 1, had an engine release road and, indeed, the locomotive which had brought the train into Exmouth, and which also appears to be an Ivatt tank, can be seen at the buffer stops. The old order can be seen on the far left in the shape of M7 tank No. 30676 parked alongside the small engine shed which was to close in November 1963. No. 41306 had been allocated to Exmouth Junction in June 1955 and was to stay in residence there until the end of 1963. In all no less than thirty-one different members of this useful class were to be allocated to 72A over the years and they proved to be able replacements for the SR's stock of ageing branch line tank locomotives. *RCR14383*

Opposite bottom: On the 13 October 1959 the signalman based at Exmouth's seventy lever box can be seen standing on one of the small projecting balconies with arm outstretched ready to hand over the single line token to a train bound for Tipton St. Johns hauled by Standard 2-6-2T No. 82017 whose driver also has his arm ready to receive the token. At Tipton connections were made with services from Sidmouth to the main line at Sidmouth Junction. The signal box dated from 1924 and was to continue in service until March 1968 when the remaining single line to Topsham came under the control of a wooden train staff held by the driver. A sharp twenty chain radius curve would greet the locomotive once past the signal box followed by a one mile climb up a 1 in 50 gradient to Littleham crossing over the Exeter road on a graceful curving viaduct now sadly demolished. The semi-detached houses in adjacent Halsdon Road had a good view of proceedings. *RCR14875*

TOPSHAM

177¼ miles from London. Served by express trains, including the "Atlantic Coast Express" from Waterloo with change of train at Exeter Central. Journey time approx. 3½ hours

Topsham is an ancient town standing on the east bank of the Exe estuary and was once a considerable port. Its winding streets and narrow lanes have interesting buildings of several different periods, perhaps the most notable being some beautiful Dutch style houses, built by refugees who fled the religious persecutions of their own country, to find a haven in this Devon port.

Top: The Topsham signalman stands at the end of the down platform ready to hand over the token for the single line onwards to Exmouth to the fireman of the approaching service consisting of three coaches and a van headed by Ivatt tank No. 41318 on 12 October 1959. Meanwhile M7 0-4-4T No. 30323, leaking copious amounts of steam, will shortly depart under clear signals for Exeter Central with a four coach set. The line northwards to Exmouth Junction had been doubled in 1908 but would revert to single track in 1973, the same year that full lifting barriers replaced the level crossing gates seen here. The signal box which can just be glimpsed behind the Drummond tank locomotive closed in January 1988 following the introduction of colour light signals but remains in situ as it received a Grade II listing the same year. *RCR14349*

Bottom: A clearer view of Topsham signal box is afforded by this shot taken from the carriage window of the 12.15pm service from Exeter Central to Exmouth, pulling in to Topsham headed by Standard tank No. 82022. Also in view is the 12.15pm service from Exmouth to Exeter with Ivatt tank No. 41308 at its head waiting to depart on 25 May 1961. The loco crews appear about to exchange a few words as their respective trains pass. The signal box contained a twenty-three lever frame and at the time of this view BR three-position signalling instruments were in use which had replaced the previous Sykes' lock and block system. Tokenless block was subsequently introduced when the line was singled in 1973. In the background is the impressive Gothic station building of 1860 to a design of Sir William Tite although its original red brick and stone features were somewhat spoiled by the later rendering applied to part of the building by the SR. *LRF5710*

BARNSTAPLE

211½ miles from London. Served by express trains, including the "Atlantic Coast Express", from Waterloo. Journey time approx. 5¼ hours. On weekdays only can also be reached by express trains from Paddington and from the North, Midlands and South Wales with a change of train at Taunton.

Barnstaple, the gateway to the scenic glories of North Devon's coast and countryside, claims to be the oldest borough in the kingdom, but it is well abreast of the times. The River Taw runs through the town, which retains many links with the past, such as the Pannier Market and Barnstaple Great Fair, held every September. The North Devon Athenaeum contains a fine library and museum. Buses connect Barnstaple with Lynton and Lynmouth, skirting the Doone country en route.

M7 No. 30023 is engaged in some light shunting at Barnstaple Junction station on 16 August 1960. A number of these Drummond tank locomotives were based at Barnstaple over the years with this example lasting in traffic here until withdrawal in October 1961. Barnstaple's final class members left in early 1963 when two of the remaining M7 trio, Nos. 30251 and 30254, departed for Feltham and Bournemouth respectively in January whilst No. 30670 was withdrawn from service the following month. The arch of the bridge seen above the second wagon carried the main road over the line to Ilfracombe whilst the third wagon is standing on the board crossing linking the main up platform with the down platforms. These platforms were also linked by the footbridge which was extended in 1924, during the conversion of the down platform into an island following the cutting back of the hillside to allow an additional track to be laid. This also provided an access to the main road for pedestrians to the developing residential area to the south of the town. *WS4936*

ILFRACOMBE

226½ miles from London. Served by express trains, including the "Atlantic Coast Express" from Waterloo. Journey time approx 6 hours. Can also be reached on weekdays only by express trains from Paddington and from the North, Midlands and South Wales with change of train at Taunton.

Ilfracombe's natural loveliness may be said to have been developed not exploited. Its winter climate is kindly but never enervating. Set in a panorama of beauty, there are marine walks bounded by sea and rock. In spite of Ilfracombe's up and down hill growth, its sandy coves are ideal for bathing and in addition the town has one of the largest covered swimming baths in the west. Ilfracombe has history. Its harbour dates from at least Saxon times, but its laudable ambition today is to ensure that its holiday visitors get such a welcome and such enjoyment that a return visit becomes an automatic certainty.

Opposite top: Carefully negotiating the severe curve, subject to a 15 mph speed restriction, into Barnstaple Junction station comes West Country No. 34033 "Chard" with the 12.20 pm service from Ilfracombe to Waterloo on 1 June 1960. The signalman from "B" box situated between the Ilfracombe and Torrington lines can be seen walking back to the steps leading up to his box clutching the recently surrendered single line token for the section across the Taw Viaduct from Barnstaple Town station. Although this had the advantage of being a through service to the capital for returning holidaymakers there were a considerable number of stops to be endured before the end of the six hour thirteen minute journey from the North Devon coastal resort. Having already called at all stations between Ilfracombe and Barnstaple Junction the train, after attaching a portion from Torrington at Barnstaple Junction, proceeded to serve all stations, except Newton St. Cyres, before reaching Exeter Central where locomotives would be changed, a buffet car and a portion from Plymouth attached. Progress was then a little faster with stops at Sidmouth Junction, Seaton Junction, Axminster, Yeovil Junction, Sherborne, Templecombe and Gillingham before Salisbury was reached. Thence just Andover Junction, Woking and Surbiton, set down only, were served before eventual arrival into Waterloo at 6.33 pm. *LRF4774*

Opposite bottom: West Country pacific No. 34108 "Wincanton", in original "air smoothed" condition, was captured on Barnstaple Junction shed, coded 72E, on 16 August 1960. The shed had no pacifics of its own allocated there but serviced those arriving from Exeter and in this view, having raked out the ashpan, the clinker from which is seen smouldering at the side of the track, the rear axlebox seems to be receiving some attention. No. 34108 was part of the Exmouth Junction shed stud of these Bulleid machines and would be modified into rebuilt form in early 1961. It lasted in traffic almost until the end of steam on the SR, being withdrawn in June 1967 before being scrapped at Buttigieg's yard in Newport having spent more than a year in the yard awaiting its eventual demise. *WS4935.*

Above: Hopefully this party of home going boy scouts have enjoyed their week's camp in the Ilfracombe area or perhaps they are setting off for camp elsewhere. No doubt their leaders will have availed themselves of BR's Party Travel facility whereby "Organised parties of juveniles, eight or more, attending camps and rallies, can obtain reduced fare tickets, available for one month, by prior arrangement." Their camping paraphernalia is probably destined for loading into the van attached to the head of the carriage rake. At the longer platform, No. 2, Maunsell N Class mogul No. 31845 is due to take out a later departure on 16 August 1958. Following extensive track improvements in 1929 the number of carriage sidings, seen on the left of this view, were increased from three to seven. *AEB3922*

Above: On 17 August 1960 Battle of Britain No. 34065 "Hurricane" awaits departure time at the bay platform with a service for Exeter whilst N Class mogul No. 31840 is acting as station pilot having shunted some coaches into the main platform. The station at Ilfracombe was perched some 250 feet above the town so taxis, which did a good trade especially on summer Saturdays, were popular for holidaymakers arriving with their luggage, this being even more necessary for returning holidaymakers in view of the steep climb up from the town. Locomotives had it no easier with a gradient of 1 in 153 at the buffer stops steepening to 1 in 71 on leaving the platform, rising to 1 in 36 for the two mile climb up the bank towards Mortehoe, necessitating double heading on the heavier trains and limiting speed to not much more than 25 mph. The Bulleids were allowed to take 205 tons unaided up the bank hence the lack of a pilot on the pacific's short train seen here. *JB034*

Opposite top: N Class mogul No. 31841 has charge of an evening service to Barnstaple Junction on 16 August 1960. These Maunsell moguls came to the line in the mid 1920s and were to prove the mainstay of motive power until the advent of the Bulleid pacifics. The statistics for Ilfracombe, in common with many another resort served by the SR, showed that 75% of its annual passenger traffic was carried in just three months of the summer period. A review undertaken in 1963 sponsored by the Dartington Hall Trustees and published as the North Devon Railway Report revealed that the Exeter to Ilfracombe line covered only 31% of its annual costs. The report also showed that Ilfracombe was heavily dependent upon the holiday trade with 25% of all visitors arriving by train. In spite of economies introduced before closure the inevitable occurred in October 1970 when the last trains ran between Ilfracombe and Barnstaple Junction. *WS4938*

Opposite bottom: Following the WR takeover of SR lines west of Wilton in 1963 modern diesels were to be seen on many parts of the former rival's empire in North Devon. Local footplatemen were trained on North British Type 2 "Baby Warships" and Hymeks with the heavy summer trains being shared between steam and diesel haulage during the final summer of through working to Waterloo in 1964. No. D7095, which was less than a year old and had recently been reallocated from Newton Abbot to Plymouth Laira depot, is seen departing from Ilfracombe on Wednesday 22 July 1964 under the watchful eye of the Ilfracombe signalman gazing from the window of his box which contained a fifty lever frame although ten were never used. This was the third such box to be provided here, the first opening with the line in 1874, a replacement opening in 1891 and the third in 1929 with closure coming in December 1967. The final "Atlantic Coast Express" arrived in Ilfracombe a few weeks later on 5 September 1964, bringing to an end through services from Waterloo and thereafter DMUs with the occasional loco hauled service operated to Exeter St. David's where connections, albeit often very poor ones, could be made for London trains to Paddington. Hymeks and Warships continued to operate the few remaining summer Saturday through trains from Ilfracombe to Paddington until eventual closure of the line in 1970. *RCR17671*

INSTOW

218 miles from London. Served by express trains, including the "Atlantic Coast Express" from Waterloo. Journey time approx. 5¾ hours.

Instow, population 785, on the North Devon coast exactly opposite Appledore, with which it is linked by a ferry across the mouth of the Torridge estuary, has miles of beautiful sands. It is an excellent place for sea and river bathing, boating and fishing. Early closing day Wednesday.

The moment of tablet exchange is captured in this shot of Ivatt tank No. 41298 passing the LSWR signal box prior to its stop at Instow station with a service from Barnstaple to Torrington. Although closure to passengers came in October 1965 and closure of the route to goods traffic followed in 1978 the thirteen lever box dating from 1872 escaped demolition and in fact became the first structure of its type to be awarded a Grade II listing. A local preservation group now looks after the box which is open to the public. The passing loop, the points controlling access to which can be seen in the foreground, was taken out of use in 1968 when the box was reduced to merely controlling the adjacent level crossing gates and associated signalling. The station was well located for the village and just a short walk to the nearby sandy beach which has long been popular with day trippers and holidaymakers alike. Although the date of this view has not been recorded it could have been as early as 1955 for No. 41298 was actually the first of the type allocated to Barnstaple Junction shed, in July 1953, staying for almost ten years until reallocated in March 1963. *REV-26-1*

Opposite top: Like Exeter St. David's station Plymouth North Road was one of those rare locations where trains heading towards London might depart in opposite directions. The interloper, in the form of Battle of Britain No. 34055 "Fighter Pilot", has just got away westwards with a London Waterloo service via Okehampton on 15 July 1956. The returning holidaymaker therefore had a choice of routes, albeit that the SR mileage from Plymouth to Waterloo was 233¾ as against the WR's 225¾ miles via Castle Cary. No. 34055 was a Salisbury based locomotive at this date so may well have been working back as far as the Wiltshire city. *RCR7693*

PLYMOUTH

231 miles from London. Served by express trains, including the "Atlantic Coast Express" from Waterloo. Journey time approx. 6 hours. Also served by express trains from Paddington.

This great port has given its name to at least 40 other towns all over the globe. Plymouth's superb situation

makes it an excellent holiday resort and centre for touring. Plymouth still functions as an ocean port and the day to day harbour traffic is often augmented by tenders going to and from a liner waiting in the Sound. Many of the old landmarks perished in the last war, but the Mayflower Stone and other monuments to a stirring past still remain. Old customs remain too, such as the ancient "Fisching Feaste" in memory of Sir Francis Drake.

Above: A rather damp 1 May 1961 sees T9 No. 30120 entering Plymouth North Road station with a three coach train which, by the WR headcode being displayed, would indicate an empty stock working probably from the SR's Friary facility. By this date this "Greyhound" had less than a year of BR service to run before being withdrawn for preservation as part of the National Collection in March 1962. *RCR15691*

Cornwall

BUDE

228½ miles from London. Served by express trains, including the "Atlantic Coast Express" from Waterloo. Journey time approx. 6 hours. Also served by expresses from the Midlands, South Wales and London Paddington with change of train at Exeter St.David's.

Tennyson's "thundering shores of Bude and Bos" is an apt description when the Atlantic is feeling fretful. But during the holiday season the ocean is usually on its best behaviour, especially at Bude. This utterly unspoilt resort has compromised with modernity to the extent of providing good shops, restaurants and cafes, and excellent holiday accommodation. There is also a large seawater swimming pool, cleaned and replenished by every tide. But there are no man made promenades, fun fairs or amusement arcades. Nothing artificial could ever compete with the rich benefits bestowed by nature on this quiet haven. Children adore Bude. Long sunny days can be spent without boredom and in perfect safety on its excellent sands. Older folk are just as happy, for at Bude there is a time to be active and a time to be still, with ample opportunities for both.

Top: Drummond's T9 "Greyhounds" served the SR's Cornish outposts for more than 30 years, the final three examples not being withdrawn until the summer of 1961. Three years earlier No. 30712 is seen at the terminus at Bude on 18 August 1958 with a service for Okehampton where connections could be made for Exeter and Plymouth. This example, dating from 1899, only had another 15 months in service before withdrawal from Exmouth Junction shed in November 1959. At this time the quickest journey from Bude to Okehampton, 31¾ miles away, took 77 minutes, giving an average speed of 24 mph. Surprisingly this was not by the Atlantic Coast Express due to the fact that passengers on that service had to endure a 16 minute wait at Halwill Junction to attach the portion from Padstow before going forward. Today a bus connection links Bude with Okehampton and Exeter St. Davids' station, the journey from Bude to Okehampton taking 65 minutes. Progress? – perhaps. *AEB3980*

Bottom: By the date of this view, 16 June 1962, the T9s were history although the preserved example No. 120 would make a return visit to the North Cornwall line in April 1963. Their replacements were Maunsell moguls and Standard tanks of both Class 4MT and Class 3MT types, one of the latter, No. 82023, being seen here backing down onto its train of two coaches and two vans standing at Bude's bay platform. Coach set No. 96 was in use being a Maunsell two coach local P set which were the mainstay of local services on the Bude, Padstow and Bodmin services. They normally consisted of a 6 compartment brake third paired with a 6 compartment brake composite and at this date the coaches in this set were Nos. 2778 (brake) and 6667 (Compo). This rake formed the last train of the day, the 7.02 pm to Halwill Junction, where a 13 minute wait gave a connection to Okehampton and where, after another 21 minutes, a connecting service could be boarded for Exeter Central, reached at 9.48 pm. A wait of 41 minutes at Okehampton would allow Plymouth to be reached. After a day on the beach in Bude such slack connections would no doubt have contributed to the unattractiveness of such services, not only to the day tripper returning to Exeter or Plymouth but to the general travelling public. The guard for the service can be seen walking in front of the locomotive with a broom carried for sweeping out his compartment perhaps. *RCR16519*

PORT ISAAC ROAD

251 miles from Waterloo. Served by express trains, including the "Atlantic Coast Express" from Waterloo. Journey time approx. 6¾ hours. Change at Port Isaac Road station for bus connection to Port Isaac.

The older part of Port Isaac is a typical Cornish fishing village packed tightly between steep hills overlooking a pier built in the reign of Henry VIII. Modern houses and hotels climb higher up the hills and cater for the increasing number of holidaymakers attracted by the extreme picturesqueness of the village.

It was a sure bet that any station ending with the suffix "Road" was going to be some distance from the settlement it aimed to serve and such was the case with Port Isaac Road on the North Cornwall line, the village lying some 4 miles away. This view taken on 12 July 1961 reveals the isolated setting of the station which was situated up a lane off the steep and narrow cross country minor road from St. Teath to Pendogget. Although a sporadic bus service linked the station and the resort, its relative inaccessibility was no doubt a factor in dissuading some holidaymakers from using the train especially with the rise in car ownership in the late 1950s and early 1960s. On the other hand the comparative isolation of this part of North Cornwall was undoubtedly the attraction for some of the more discerning clientele. BR undertook several surveys of usage of the line and that of July 1963, for example, revealed that a daily average of just 5 passengers joined trains here whilst 12 alighted on Mondays-Fridays, rising to 25 joining and 34 alighting on Saturdays. When it is considered that the station was served by 5 trains in each direction on Mondays-Fridays and 7 westbound and 6 eastbound on Saturdays the average per train was very low. Usage outside the holiday season was even worse as a survey undertaken in March 1964 showed when it revealed a daily average of just 4 passengers joining and 4 alighting on Mondays-Fridays. It was really no surprise that such levels of patronage could not be sustained and that the line closed in October 1966. *RCR16077*

WADEBRIDGE

254 miles from London. Served by express trains including the "Atlantic Coast Express" from Waterloo. Journey time approx. 6½ hours.

Wadebridge, on the banks of the River Camel, has a medieval bridge of seventeen arches spanning the river. It is, of course, a centre par excellence for the King Arthur country, the coastline glories of north Cornwall and the Cornish moors. It is also a good junction point for Padstow, Newquay and Bodmin. Bowling, tennis and bathing are among the local diversions and indoor amusement is also catered for.

Above: Typifying the SR's penchant for multi-portioned trains, the 12.58pm from Padstow rolls into Wadebridge behind N mogul No. 31831 on 16 July 1958. This will form the 1.12pm departure all stations to Okehampton where, having already been joined by a portion from Bude at Halwill Junction, it will be joined to a portion from Plymouth going forward to Exeter Central. Here a portion from Torrington, which will have joined a portion from Ilfracombe at Barnstaple Junction, will be attached plus a restaurant car for the onward journey to Waterloo. Whilst through carriages were no doubt much appreciated by the holidaymaking public, removing the necessity for carting luggage from one train to another, the downside was the inherent delay introduced into the overall journey by the coupling and uncoupling of carriage portions. No. 31831 was based at Exmouth Junction shed for the majority of the 1950s, remaining there until transfer right across the country to Brighton in October 1962. *AS-D76-2*

Opposite top: Whilst the fireman of T9 No. 30338 rakes some coal forward in the tender, the driver mounts the footplate for the onward journey with the 9.56 am service from Okehampton to Padstow on 4 June 1960. This service, which had stopped at every station on the North Cornwall line, was due into Wadebridge at 11.56, exactly 2 hours after leaving Okehampton 56½ miles away. The former Poet Laureate John Betjeman famously recorded his impression of alighting at Wadebridge station whilst journeying to the family holiday home at Trebetherick in his 1960 verse autobiography "Summoned by Bells". Today of course the old station building does duty as the John Betjeman Centre, a hub for local senior citizens, whilst a road appropriately named Southern Way runs where this Greyhound once stood. *LRF4943*

Opposite bottom: A lull in proceedings in the shed yard on the 22 June 1962 reveals a shunter with his pole taking a well earned break alongside the coal stacks whilst one of the crew of Collett pannier tank No. 1368 glances from his cab. No. 1368 had arrived in Wadebridge a couple of months previously, having been ousted from Weymouth Docks by dieselisation, in order to test the suitability of the class as replacements for the ageing Beattie well tanks. The trial proved successful and No. 1368 was followed by a couple more of the same class in August 1962. One of the soon to be ousted Beatties in the form of No. 30586 is on the left whilst N Class mogul No. 31875 completes the scene. *RCR16576*

Southern to the Coast

PADSTOW

259¾ miles from London. Served by express trains including the "Atlantic Coast Express" from Waterloo. Journey time approx. 6¾ hours. Refreshment Car on most trains.

Padstow is an ancient seaport on the lovely estuary of the River Camel backed by gentle wooded hills. Once an important shipbuilding town, it has retained many of its medieval aspects and traditions, for instance, the Hobby Horse parade. The estuary, as it widens towards the sea, has many small sandy coves popular for picnics. Population of Padstow and Trevone is 2,852. Early closing day Wednesday.

Top: It was not always a diet of T9s at Padstow, variety in the motive power being provided by, amongst others, the Adams O2 tanks which operated services to Bodmin North. No. 30236 of this class is seen running round its train before returning to Bodmin on 16 July 1958. Apart from a brief push-pull interlude in 1918 this manoeuvre was necessary at both Padstow and Bodmin North and of course at Wadebridge where short workings were involved. Wadebridge usually had a couple of these 0-4-4Ts on their books and at the date of this view the other example was No. 30200. Variety was also provided by Bulleid pacifics, Maunsell moguls, GWR 45XX tank locomotives which visited twice daily on services from Bodmin Road and even the occasional Beattie well tank. The final O2 based at Wadebridge would depart in March 1961, No. 30236, seen here, having been withdrawn in January 1960. Their replacements came in the form of 57XX pannier tanks Nos. 3633, 3679, 4666 and 4694. AS D75-4

Bottom: Our final shot of a Greyhound, No. 30710, is at Padstow awaiting time with the 12.58pm departure to Waterloo also on 16 July 1958. Having brought in the 9.56 from Okehampton and turned on the 70 foot turntable it will power this train only as far as Wadebridge where it will hand over to a Maunsell mogul. The brooding presence of what was the Metropole Hotel, which had been completed at the start of the 20th.c by a Cardiff shipowner at a cost of £12,000 (£1.5m in today's money), can be seen above the station canopy in the left background. Although known as the South Western hotel, before a name change to the Metropole, it was never in fact owned by the railway, the name probably relating to the area of the south west rather than to the railway company. The hotel was sold to Trust House Forte in 1936 and was requisitioned by the Admiralty during World War II. Today it is known as the Padstow Harbour, "a recently renovated Victorian boutique hotel". Describing itself in contemporary advertisements soon after opening as a "First Class Family Hotel, handsomely furnished, very commodious and an ideal Summer and Winter residence", it attracted many "high class" visitors to make the long journey from London and elsewhere by train, being situated as it was conveniently near to the station. The Prince of Wales visited in the 1930s in order to play golf on the local courses whilst influxes of day trippers from as far afield as Exeter were also good patrons of the railway as they were able to spend 7 hours or so in the resort at the time of this view providing of course that you were willing to endure the 7 or 8 hours on the outward and return journeys. AS D76-1